# The Horse of My Dreams

## True Stories of the HORSES WE LOVE

### EDITED BY
## Callie Smith Grant

Revell

a division of Baker Publishing Group
Grand Rapids, Michigan

© 2019 by Baker Publishing Group

Published by Revell
a division of Baker Publishing Group
PO Box 6287, Grand Rapids, MI 49516-6287
www.revellbooks.com

Printed in the United States of America

Library of Congress Cataloging-in-Publication Data
Names: Grant, Callie Smith, editor.
Title: The horse of my dreams : true stories of the horses we love / Callie Smith
    Grant, ed.
Description: Grand Rapids : Revell, a division of Baker Publishing Group, [2019] |
    Includes bibliographical references.
Identifiers: LCCN 2019002512 | ISBN 9780800727185 (paperback)
Subjects: LCSH: Horses—Anecdotes. | Horse owners—Anecdotes. |
    Horsemanship—Anecdotes. | Human-animal relationships—Anecdotes.
Classification: LCC SF301 .H66 2019 | DDC 636.1—dc23
LC record available at https://lccn.loc.gov/2019002512

19  20  21  22  23  24  25        7  6  5  4  3  2  1

In keeping with biblical principles of creation stewardship, Baker Publishing Group advocates the responsible use of our natural resources. As a member of the Green Press Initiative, our company uses recycled paper when possible. The text paper of this book is composed in part of post-consumer waste.

To the memory of Jeanette Marie Thomason
Encourager, lover of words, rescuer of horses from wildfires . . .
and gone too soon.
Rest in peace, my friend.

# Contents

# Contents

# Contents

# Introduction

## Callie Smith Grant

Many years ago my husband made a promise to take me on a trip to the California desert. The desert had always extended a strange pull on me, but although we lived in California for many years, I had not seen either the Mojave Desert or Death Valley. So the day finally came when we took time off work, packed our car with cases of water, and drove to the Mojave Desert when the wildflowers were in bloom. Then we drove into Death Valley, a place I found as strange as another planet and more beautiful than I could even imagine.

Death Valley held another surprise for me—a herd of wild horses. We watched them gallop through the sand near Death Valley Junction and huddle up to somebody's backyard fence. I loved their sturdy bodies, their wild yet still precise way of moving together as a herd, their sweet approach at the fence. I recall that some of their eyelashes were caked in sand. I've always wanted to go back and find the wild herd again—and maybe someday I will. For now, that herd at times shows up in my sleep, running over a sandy expanse in my dreams.

Of course, there's another kind of dream of horses, one that's grounded in waking reality. It's the dream of having a horse of one's own. A lot of people have this dream, and some are blessed to have it fulfilled. This book is full of such people and their dreams and their horses. Some of these dreams came true in childhood, some during teenage years, some in middle age, and some, as one writer put it, "well north of sixty years old." A couple of the horse dreams never came true in the flesh, but that love of horses played a strong and positive part in their lives anyway.

In these stories, you'll meet a gorgeous variety of horses, ponies, and even two adorable donkeys. They are old and young, large and lean, and they desire to belong, whether their herd is human or animal. These horses are owned, borrowed, worked for, admired from afar, or simply remembered. They may show up at the right time—and sometimes they show up at the wrong time (or did they?). In these stories, horses empower children. They help the elderly adjust to changes. They join a family and help them get through a tough time. Sometimes they come alongside a person to help him or her make a living. They assist the anxious or depressed and in the process affirm to them that a loving Creator is present. Sometimes they make humans laugh. Often they are simply someone's best friend.

There are horse lovers within these pages who understand a horse's moves and intentions and desires. There are others who view the unique thinking of this creature as hard to understand. But when that animal intelligence meets up with our human intelligence, wonderful things can happen. And stories are born.

Obviously the stories in this book have the love for horses in common. But they often also have hope in common. I was surprised to see how many contributors wrote specifically about their dream of having a horse—using that very phrase—and because of that, this collection pretty much titled itself. Contributors wrote from their hearts, their memories, their longings, their joys, and that common theme—"the horse of my dreams"—floated to the top. It was as if some of these horse lovers connected with each other even before the conception of this book. To me, a person with a lucid dream world, it made perfect sense.

Shakespeare helps us understand why horses invade our dreams and our lives: "He is pure air and fire; and the dull elements of earth and water never appear in him, but only in patient stillness while his rider mounts him. He is indeed a horse, and all other jades you may call beasts."[1]

I know you'll enjoy meeting these beautiful creatures and their humans in these true stories of *The Horse of My Dreams*. And may you also enjoy the horse of *your* dreams in any way you can.

# When Stubborn Meets Stubborn

## *Lauraine Snelling*

A pony!" I stared at the Shetland pony backing out of a trailer right in our yard. "For me?"

When I got excited, I would rub my clenched hands together and scrunch my face in a grin. I added jigging in place that night.

The man handed my dad the lead tied to the pony's halter. "Her name is Polly, and she's pretty old, but she'll be a good first pony for your little girl." He smiled at me standing by my mother. "You got a bridle or saddle?"

Daddy shook his head.

The man reached in the trailer and unhooked a bridle. "I'll pick this up sometime when I'm nearby. Oh, and Polly likes sugar cubes. I don't give her many, not good for her teeth, but she loves them."

"Thank you." Daddy and the man shook hands, then the man got in his truck and drove off. But I didn't watch that. All I could see was a pony who looked grizzled gray in the fading light. Dusk was creeping across the land, the cows were milked and chores done. A good time for a pony to arrive.

But when wasn't a good time for a pony?

I stood in front of her and just stared. My pony was a dream of a lifetime. Even at five, I had wanted a pony for what felt like forever. Polly nibbled at my fingers when I reached out to stroke her face, making me giggle.

Mom returned from the house and handed me a couple of sugar cubes. My dad liked to dunk a sugar cube in his coffee, just like his pa did.

"Give it to her on the flat of your hand," Daddy said. "She might be old, but if she mistakes your fingers for a sugar cube . . ."

I nodded and did as told, giggling when her whiskers tickled my palm. "She likes it, all right." I let her finish and held out the other.

"I'll bridle her up and then you can ride."

"Really?"

He looped the rope around Polly's neck and unbuckled the halter. "She might try to take off on you, so don't give her a chance." Polly took the bit without an argument, and he buckled the bridle in place. "Watch how to do this so you can do it yourself next time."

I nodded, and everything seemed to happen in slow motion. Polly swished her tail and stamped one front foot.

"Now, here you go. Hang on to the reins." Like most farm kids, I had ridden on our team of workhorses, but I'd never ridden my own pony. Daddy picked me up and set me on her back, reins in hand. He slapped Polly on the rump, and she took off, and I did too, only in the opposite direction, screaming all the while.

I don't know how my dad caught her. I would always need a can of oats to bribe her with, but he caught her, set me up on her back again, and said, "Now hang on." That was the best advice my father ever gave me. Hang on. And so began my years with Polly.

The dream had started some time before. When you are little, ten minutes can seem like forever. "Mommy, when we get to the farm, can I have a pony?" I had asked her.

"We shall see."

I studied her face. That was one of those puzzling lines along with "maybe." I have no idea when I started wanting a pony, but ponies and town living didn't mix. But now we were in Minnesota, where my daddy had grown up before going into the navy. The war was over, and he was hoping to buy a dairy farm. A farm meant land and pasture for a pony. And lots of cows, which suited me fine, animal lover that I already was. We had a dog—a rat terrier—but a farm meant cows and horses and chickens, maybe pigs also. Surely we would have cats in the barn and in the house too.

The farm we moved to had a big white barn with stanchions for the cows on both sides of the center aisle down the length and box stalls at either end. A silo guarded the barn and long machine shed. We had a two-story house where the upstairs was divided into two bedrooms with slanted ceilings that made it seem cozier. My mom and dad had a bedroom downstairs. A black cast-iron cookstove dominated the kitchen and provided heat for the house.

After our first rather surprising evening, Polly and I slowly became friends. She was an opinionated creature who did not like to be ordered around. She had lived many years and knew every trick in *The Book of Shetland Pony Behaviors*.

**The Book**

1. You do not come when called. You wait until you hear the oats rattling in the can. No oats in the can, you do not get caught.
2. You do not stand still the first time when your girl tries to get on your back. A handful of oats is the price.

3. If you do not feel the terrain is solid, no amount of leg banging and orders will persuade you. The best thing to do is whirl around and run for the barn.

4. When your girl wants to ride to her friend's house, you go as far as you feel like, then whirl and head for the barn. If the barn door is closed, you wheel and head for the gate. Stop as abruptly as possible.

5. If your rider happens to fall off, head for the barn.

6. If she yells at you, ignore her. She'll get over it.

7. Do not bite. Biting is bad pony manners.

8. After your girl has brushed you and sprayed you with water, go roll in the dusty place where all the horses roll.

I learned that even if I was in a bit of a hurry, I worked by her rules—or else. Polly did not like to be rushed. But I also learned how to work around her.

Take her not wanting to go away from the farm. I would mount by the lowest rail on the pole bar gate and cluck her into moving. I'd talk to her and pat her neck. The county road made a gentle ninety-degree turn on the other side of the farm fence in the corner of the section where the barn stood. On a good day we would trot out, round the corner, and start up to my friend Florence's house.

The road went down a short way and up a gentle hill to the next county road that bordered the west side of our farm. Turn left on that road, and Florence's farmhouse was a couple hundred feet away. Not a long ride by any means. I clutched the rope that worked as reins tied to Polly's halter and watched her ears. I'd keep talking to her, telling her how good she was being, and keep my bare legs ready for action. As soon as she tightened to turn, I bailed off, making sure to hang on to the reins. Then I dragged her the rest of the way to Florence's house. Sometimes I ended up in the dirt, but I kept getting better.

When it was time to go home, I would mount up, trot out to the road, and hang on while Polly went on a dead run clear to our barn. At our driveway she would hook a sharp left and plow to a stop at the barn. In those Bemidji summers, she would be dripping with sweat, and so would I. We girls only wore dresses then, and my long legs were strong from hanging on to Polly and itchy from riding a sweaty pony.

I remember my mother telling me years later that the mailman used to drive behind me, and did they know how Polly and I did not look both ways before charging across the road? He also said I clung like a burr to that pony's back. Desperation is a good teacher. Determination too.

Two summers later we moved to another farm in Solway, Minnesota, which might as well have been a world away for Florence and me. Since we were farming with milking cows, we didn't do a lot of visiting, and when we did it was mostly into Bemidji, where my relatives lived. I'm not sure I ever saw Florence again, though we did write letters to each other, and I think it was in the next year that she died from cancer. When you are seven years old, that seems incomprehensible. Now as an adult, it still does.

I remember my cousins coming out to the farm, and my boy cousins planning to show me how to make Polly mind. Right. She wasn't very tall, but oh my, she was strong. When she whirled and tore out, they did the same thing I did that first night we had her. I always told them what Daddy told me: *Hang on.*

When my cousins came, we'd make ice cream in the crank freezer. We'd put a cake of ice in a gunny sack and slam the broad side of the axe against the sack until the ice was usable. Then we'd pour those ice chips into the crank machine. That was the best ice cream ever.

We had no electricity at that house, so we used kerosene lamps and lanterns and a big black wood cookstove. We milked the cows by hand and ran the milk through the separator, a machine of many cones that needed to be washed very carefully. That was one of my jobs.

Those summers Polly and I also became babysitters. While Mom and Dad worked the fields, hayed, and kept the farm going, I was in charge of my little brother and baby sister. They both loved to ride Polly, so I would put them on her back and lead her around. One time Polly stumbled, and Karen fell off and got up with a bruise on her cheek. I figured I was in for it then. But the bruise hardly showed, and my folks understood accidents.

During the winter, we kept all our animals in the barn and let them out on nice days. Polly had her own stall. When I'd walk home from the bus stop, I'd stop at the house, leave my books, change my coat, and go out to the barn to see Polly. I rigged a harness for her so she could pull the sled with Don and Karen on it. You could conquer worlds with baling twine, including creating a harness—I braided twine for reins to go with that aging halter. I'd get oats in the can when I came into the barn, and when I shook it, Polly and the gray Percherons from Daddy's work team, Flossie and Myrtle, always nickered.

I came home from school one winter day to learn that Polly had died in her stall during the night. I understood that she was a very old pony, but she'd not been sick or given us any indications. Daddy figured she was forty-one when she died.

Those last years of her life, Polly gave one little girl many happy memories and provided hours of joy and companionship. More important than the memories were the life lessons she taught me. We all need to learn how to hang on to get through this life. Now when I speak before groups of all sizes, I tell people that the best advice my father ever gave me was "Just hang on!"

# The Power of Perception

## Sarah Barnum

Twenty-five horses trot with tails streaming and hooves hammering as I push the herd from the nether regions of the pasture toward the catch pen. Every morning is the same: whistle, crack the whip, get the lead mare moving, and jump on the ATV, hoping the herd doesn't decide to go in the wrong direction. Though it's only 7:30 a.m., the summer sun has already crested the hill, bringing out a sheen of sweat on my face and promising another hundred-degree day.

I am head wrangler at a horse camp, and my day holds sweat, dust, horsehair, flies, manure, and exhaustion. But it also includes six wonderful coworkers, beautiful horses, and precious kids. By the end of the day, my voice will be hoarse from teaching and answering a million questions.

*Why is that horse blindfolded?*

That's a fly mask; the horse can see through it.

*Why does Darla have all that hair on her legs?*

She's a Clydesdale, so she has "feathers" on her legs.

*Do we get to gallop today?*

No, but you'll get to trot.

Still, I love my job.

Eleven bay-colored horses reside in the herd: brown, brown, and more brown. The students often mix them up, and even the wranglers occasionally put Destin's saddle on Gallivant by mistake. To the average observer, the bays seem indistinguishable. A brown-haired girl myself, I think that's like saying all brunettes look the same. Upon closer acquaintance, the horses are worlds different. Destin is a pink-nosed pony while Gallivant is an angular Arabian. Stetson is an old-timer quarter horse whose coat glows with red highlights, while Breyer is a boss at feeding time. Mark is a motivated Morgan, Callie a melancholy supermodel.

And then there's Uh-Oh.

Uh-Oh was born here when the camp used to be a working cattle ranch and breeding program. The stud was named Kay-Oh, and most of his progeny also inherited part of his name. I guess Uh-Oh was the unlucky one. A few of the foals grew up and became part of the lesson program, including this brown long-backed mare.

Once the herd reaches the barn, I park the ATV and then halter Uh-Oh, along with the nine other horses we'll be using for this morning's lesson. She flattens her ears and sends me a nasty look as I gently tighten the cinch. Soon the kids, a group of fifth graders, are clamoring at the gate. Once everyone has their helmets on, they line up at the loading dock—a long mounting platform. I begin assigning mounts.

"Emily, you are going to ride Gypsy—the black-and-white horse, third on the right. James, you're going to ride Scooter—the chestnut horse, second on the left. Heather, you're going to ride Uh-Oh—the bay mare at the end, on the right."

Right on cue, Heather pales with uncertainty. The adult chaperones chuckle nervously. The other kids nudge the unlucky individual, drawling out "Uhhh-Ohhh" in mocking tones. I launch into my well-worn explanation.

"Registered horses are usually named after their sire or dam. Uh-Oh is named after her father, Kay-Oh . . ."

But the damage is already done, and I'm getting tired of trying to explain away the fear. I can practically see the power of perception taking hold in Heather. She's instantly afraid and now expects Uh-Oh to misbehave. This paralyzing timidity allows Uh-Oh to take advantage of her rider. And take advantage she does.

We make it into the arena, and when the horses begin circling the perimeter, Uh-Oh is already crowding the horse in front of her, her buddy Payday, a chubby gray gelding. She tosses her head when Heather pulls back on the reins, becoming more easily frustrated and impatient than the other horses with the mistakes their beginner riders make. When it's time for a short trot, Uh-Oh breaks into a lope instead.

"Pull back!" I call.

But Heather is too busy clinging to the saddle horn to follow my instruction or do anything with the reins. Fortunately, my assistant Aimee is waiting in the corner of the ring and grabs a rein to slow her down—wide-eyed passenger still intact. I breathe a sigh of relief. Uh-Oh never does anything dangerous like buck or rear, but the little things worry me.

It's time for an intervention.

After the lesson with Heather, I start Uh-Oh back in boot camp, pulling her out of the lesson rotation and making extra time to work her. First up: some sessions in the arena. After I mount, she pulls a few evasive measures from her bag of tricks, but I quickly block and discipline her behavior. When she throws her head, I hold my hands steady until she softens to the bit. When she goes too fast, I circle her until she trots on a loose rein. Finally, she settles down to work.

Next, I deal with her separation anxiety at what I dub "the tantrum tree." After I tie her there alone, Uh-Oh's piercing whinny trumpets through the clear air, calling to her friends. She tramples the weeds around the old oak with her fretful pawing. Once Uh-Oh maintains some sanity while separated from the herd, we progress to confidence-building trail rides on short trips away from the barn. Uh-Oh no doubt considers it more of a psychological torture session. She quivers as we set out on our own, her ears swiveling like radar sensors to catch every sound. I can see the sparks flying from the wiring in her brain as she struggles with the age-old battle of instinct versus obedience.

After some time together, I see improvement. As always, more relationship brings empathy and better understanding. With a bit of remedial maintenance, there is a well-trained, pleasurable horse underneath the bad habits.

But there is still the matter of her name.

I believe that words and names powerfully shape attitudes and identities. Uh-Oh's name has certainly shaped hers. Of all the horses in the herd, she has been the most accident-prone. An old, jagged barbed-wire scar stretches across her chest. She throws shoes regularly. On more than one occasion, I have found her head tied to the ground by a lead rope twisted around one foreleg.

Uh-Oh needs a new name. I christen her "Mellow," a confidence-inspiring name, if there ever was one. With the similar "oh" sound, it isn't difficult to make the switch.

I find my own perception of her changing. I have more patience with her. Instead of pessimistically planning for the worst, I anticipate the best. Instead of viewing her as a troublemaker, I see the responsibility as mine to find the root of the problem behaviors, correct her habits, and make sure she is comfortable and prepared. Sometimes I spend a few minutes before lessons praying over her and murmuring words like *tolerant*, *cooperative*, and *relaxed* into her ear to remind her of the privilege she has in carrying these kids.

Though she isn't perfect, with this fresh start Mellow begins to live up to her new name. The best indication is that she doesn't stand out from the group. At the end of a day of lessons, I realize that she hasn't caused any "Pull back!" moments. Or I'll notice how smoothly a class goes because she maintains good spacing with the other horses. She doesn't monopolize my assistant with her need for a constant eye.

The students who ride her are more confident—simply because of her name.

The next time I assign Mellow at the loading dock, the adults coo, "Awww, Mellow," and the other students say, "You're so lucky you got Mellow! She must be a good horse."

And she is.

# The Year of the Dream Horse

## Lisa Begin-Kruysman

My childhood home was perched on a high hilltop in the city of Hackensack, New Jersey. The house rose from a street called Longview Avenue, so named because its location afforded a glittery panoramic view of New York City and surrounding urban sprawl. As a kid, I loved to watch that famous skyline come to life in the evening from my bedroom window. Tiny beads of light shimmered on the outlines of the roads and bridges that linked all of us to the greatest city in the world.

I call my former home "Our Menagerie on the Hill," because throughout the decades, many creatures great and small made it their home. Animals featuring fur, feathers, fins, or fangs found their way into our house and hearts. I was the designated rabbit, rodent, bird, and dog person, my brother John took fish and reptile honors, and my brother Matt was our "cat guy." My sister, Manette, despite our city-like surroundings, had become obsessed with horses after she'd befriended someone who lived on a small ranch in a remote part of our county.

Subsequently, Manette's desire for a horse of her own began to haunt her dreams. One morning she came to me with a special request. It seemed she'd dreamed that a horse really did exist somewhere in our neighborhood, and she required my help finding this horse of her dreams. Only nine at the time, she needed someone older, even by a year, to accompany her as she went door-to-door asking homeowners if a horse was living in their basement.

I reluctantly agreed to go with her and was surprised to find that some people actually humored her·by letting us take a look in their cellars in the event they weren't aware that a horse inhabited their home. But as the afternoon went on, my sister grew despondent. Alas, there was no dream horse hiding in any house in our hilltop neighborhood. My sister's horse hopes dwindled as the sun set on that hot summer day.

A few years later, however, in the summer of 1973, an event occurred that offered my sister new hope. "We'll be moving to Boulder, Colorado," my parents announced. Soon, we'd all be driving from Hackensack to Boulder, where we'd live for nine months while my father enjoyed a teaching sabbatical at the University of Colorado.

We all reacted differently to this news. As far as I was concerned, this was not a good turn of events because that fall I'd been looking forward to entering the hallowed halls of Hackensack High School. I wanted no part of being a new kid at some junior high school in a town named for a huge rock somewhere in the Wild Wild West. My brothers, ages six and ten, were too young to care, but Manette was elated. Colorado was horse country. "I can finally get my own horse," she declared.

On a late August day, my entire family and our hyper toy poodle named Coco Puff set out in the family station wagon on Route

80 West on a three-day journey to Boulder. The novelty of silos, barns, and farm animals grazing in pastures soon faded. With our windows hand-cranked down, the stifling Midwestern heat enveloped us in the back of our station wagon. But despite the nonstop sibling bickering and the noxious fumes emitted by our gassy poodle, the voyage was going pretty well.

Just an hour or so outside of Boulder, however, a truck hauling a double-wide mobile home crossed over into our lane. At the wheel, my mother tried her best to keep our car on the road as it was broadsided several times. Our car careened over a wide grassy median and came to a full stop inches from crossing over into eastbound traffic.

What occurred in just moments felt like a horrifying eternity. Cars pulled over from all directions; people rushed to help. My parents called out to each of us to confirm that we were all okay. Our station wagon was totaled, and first responders later told my parents that they hadn't expected to find survivors when they arrived on the scene.

Because we had moved from New Jersey so quickly, my parents hadn't yet secured housing for us in Boulder. Now we were homeless and carless. A state trooper offered to take us to Boulder in his police cruiser. My brothers thought this was cool, but not me. Entering Boulder city limits, I slumped deep down in the big back seat of that cruiser, mortified at the prospect that one of my future classmates might catch a glimpse of our inexplicable police-escorted entrance. While I was concerned about things like first impressions and our family's lack of living arrangements in a strange new town where we knew no one, my sister had only one burning question: "When can I get a horse?"

We spent the next two nights at a motel while my parents took care of insurance matters and began to look into rental housing in Boulder. They even visited the truck driver, who'd been hospitalized with injuries he'd sustained in the accident.

Within twenty-four hours, my parents answered an ad for a house rental that clearly stated "no children or pets allowed." Because the property's details sounded so perfect for us, and because we were in such a desperate state of affairs, my parents made an appointment to see it. What did they have to lose?

When we pulled into the house's driveway, we were instructed to remain quiet in the car and to hide the dog. Before long, my parents returned to the car accompanied by the landlord. Somehow, they'd managed to convince the homeowner to change his policy. "It's okay, kids, you can come out now," they reassured us. "We have a new home." Coco barked happily and jumped out of the car to christen the lawn of her new yard in typical dog fashion.

Much to my sister's delight, this sprawling ranch home, located at the base of the Rocky Mountain foothills, came with a horse stable surrounded by several acres of fenced-in pasture. Her plan took on a new urgency; a horse must be found to complete this dream-like scenario.

After her first day in her new school, Manette rushed home filled with the exciting news that she'd be fostering a horse named Muna. The next day, she brought home a stunning gray Arabian mix. The sleek young horse's tail was held high as she gracefully trotted by us. She seemed filled with spunk and confidence despite the circumstances that had brought her into my sister's life.

Muna belonged to my sister's classmate. The horse had been injured with an axe handle by an abusive human and required a safe haven. In exchange for free boarding, Muna's owner provided food and supplies. My sister thought that was a dreamy deal.

A powerful human-horse bond quickly developed between the horse and Manette, but I couldn't say the same for me. While I admired this beautiful creature, I feared her. Muscular, strong, and willful, Muna seemed to sense my apprehension and enjoyed teasing me. While I aimed to keep my distance, my sister encouraged me to overcome my fear.

After a quick instructional demonstration, my sister commanded, "Here, saddle her up," leaving me alone to bond with Muna. But each time I tried to saddle her, Muna bared her teeth and stretched her long face in my direction, pretending to bite me.

"Don't let her get away with that!" my sister yelled when she caught her in the act. But each time I was left alone with Muna, the "game" went on again, and although she never actually sank her teeth into me, I gave up learning the art of saddling a horse.

On another occasion when I was allowed to lead the horse onto the road, Muna's backside touched a low-hanging clothesline. This spooked her; she reared up on her hind legs, wildly whinnying and thrashing her front legs in the air. Manette went into horse whisperer mode, calming the dramatic creature.

That was the end of my horse handling days.

When not off trail riding with other horse-loving friends, Manette reveled in all aspects of equine care. Feeding, grooming, even ridding the mouse-infested stable of horse manure brought her pleasure. She seemed to live in her horse-care uniform, a green long-sleeved T-shirt and overalls. At dinner, her attire filled our table with the aroma of horse barn.

But while she spent too much time with her dream horse, my sister's grades became a nightmare, and her horse privileges were in jeopardy of being revoked. When her grades didn't improve, she and a friend took a pen and changed Manette's Cs to Bs and a D to a B. Despite the fact that our father possessed two master's degrees in education, Manette somehow got away without him detecting these alterations. Later, she told me that her plan backfired because she had to work harder to keep those altered grades up, realizing that it was unlikely she'd get away with it again.

In late May, it was time for our family to say good-bye to Boulder and head back to Hackensack. And it was time for Manette to say farewell to her beloved Muna, something she did with a heavy heart. I can't imagine how hard it must have been for her to relinquish the care of her beloved horse and be concerned that she'd find another safe haven.

Again we loaded up our family wagon. A mile or so out of town, my parents spotted a horse being led by a young girl. As we got nearer, my father slowed, and my sister rolled down the car's back window to shout to her friend as she led Muna to her new home. Hearing my sister's voice, Muna threw her head back and whinnied with excitement before pushing her entire muzzle through the open window to nuzzle my sister and even our dog, who had befriended her. We all said our reluctant good-byes, and as we drove away, my sister kept her eyes fixed on the horse until the animal was no longer in view.

For a time, Manette and Muna's owner kept in touch. But my sister would never have another horse, although she never stopped dreaming of the possibility. Those many years ago, she had found herself with a purpose in a faraway place, fostering a horse in need of protection, restoring Muna's confidence in the kindness of humans. The horse in turn fulfilled the cherished dream of a young girl, if only for that year.

# Redeeming Trust

## *Cynthia Beach*

I awoke.

Sky had replaced ceiling. Why was I outdoors—and on my back—in the hill orchard? I must have walked the hill above the pasture where I boarded my fiery red gelding and, strangely, taken a nap. But why nap here? No. Something wasn't right.

Then into my sluggish mind throbbed pain. Something sticky ran down my left cheek. I raised my hand. Strange. Pebbles pressed into my palm. I picked them out before touching my face. Red crusted my fingertips. Blood. Was it mine?

Days would pass before I could remember the bareback ride where Chicobi ran downhill through the plum orchard while I clutched his back. He raked me through two trees before my head hit a limb. Seventy-two stitches, plastic surgery, and a three-day hospital stay followed. My spring break trip to Disneyland? Canceled. My seventh-grade classes—missed. Instead, I lay in bed at home, my head wrapped like a mummy's. I would wear an L-shaped scar by my left ear for life.

Two weeks after the accident, Mom and my sister Laura packed me in the car to drive five miles to the stables. Laura haltered Chicobi and led him to me. With my concussion, I still felt like I was standing on sea waves. Chicobi seemed unchanged. His muzzle was soft like warm flannel, his liquid brown eyes alert.

But me? I was changed. He could have killed me. Maybe as a young teen, I shouldn't have been on him bareback. Maybe it was my fault. Maybe it was his. I stroked him apprehensively. Within me now, etched on my soul, was a new and invisible scar. Fear had twisted the foundational thing needed in any relationship—trust. And fear had cracked this relationship that I particularly cherished—my relationship with Chicobi.

Should I sell him and get a different horse? I'm sure Mom and Dad talked about this, although I no longer recall that conversation. What I do know is that they didn't drop an ultimatum and I didn't request a different horse.

The relational repair between Chicobs and me required years. I experienced steps forward and steps backward in building trust with my horse. For years, I could ride at a walk with no fear. Anything faster, though? Sweat beaded my palms.

Two memorable events secured the final repairs in our relationship.

Years passed. Laura had graduated from college and married. And since Mom did all the horse care when we were at college, our season of horse ownership was ending. In what seemed a wonderful deal, Mom and Dad gave our horses, Chicobi and Kawiki, to the camp where Laura was now on staff. And another bonus: I would be there that summer as a canoe instructor. We could ride our horses whenever. It seemed perfect.

Then to our horror, both horses fell ill with equine distemper, also known as the strangles. No protocol had been used to protect our horses when they entered the camp herd, and our isolated horses were vulnerable in ways we didn't realize. With the strangles, horses' lymph nodes swell to the point of suffocating the animal. Unfortunately, Kawiki, Laura's mare, quickly succumbed.

A few weeks later, I arrived at camp, warned that Chicobi was very ill. In a pasture with two Belgians, he stood, his head low. His red coat had lost its fire. His throat appeared swollen and bumpy, and his hips and ribs showed. I talked to him quietly. He responded in his old familiar way. He nuzzled me.

My lips pressed together. Determination surged through me. I was going to see my horse through this.

The next day, a kind brown-haired vet coached me in caring for Chicobs. *Clean the abscesses. Don't ride. Give him these meds.* When the vet said he'd return in a few days, I fully understood how very ill Chicobs was.

Mornings and afternoons, I began a determined ritual of caring for Chicobi. I gently swabbed his abscesses. I gave him meds and readied him for repeated vet visits. On other days, I'd love on him and brush his dull coat. Our time became about being together. He responded in small ways. His head would turn; his ears would prick. I understood. Chicobi was telling me that he was grateful.

But his energy stayed low. So, day after day, I moved through the steps as fervently as a religious ritual. Then I'd soothe him, I hoped, with the soft brush and fly spray as I willed him back to health.

Five weeks passed. By July's end, the vet suggested that I start taking Chicobi on walks. Still—no riding, but I could lead him. Excitedly I strapped his apple red halter over his head and grasped the nylon lead rope. We ambled beyond the pasture gate. One afternoon we headed down the dusty dirt road along the camp. On another, we explored the archery range.

As August gained its footing and leaves started to fade, we walked farther and farther. A trail through the oak forest took us to the start of the camp's backlands—four hundred acres that we had never explored. But as we took our gentle excursions, Chicobi's ears would lift; his head too. His energy stirred. I could see his improvement.

And then.

On the eve of heading home to ready for my senior year, the vet okayed a ride. A ride! It would be our first—and only—ride of the summer.

I saddled Chicobi slowly, letting him snuffle the blanket. His weight loss forced me to hike up the cinch beyond the deep crease that marked his prior weight. He accepted the bridle and bit. Soon I was leading him outside the pasture.

I pushed my boot into the close stirrup and swung up as the music of the creaking leather sounded. My heart thudded with joy. Chicobi's ears pricked forward. I felt his ready walk. We followed the forest trail to the backlands and stood, together, on a hill to survey acre upon acre of forested land. Chicobi's ears framed the wide vista, and I remembered my old conviction: Everything's more beautiful framed between the ears of a horse.

I breathed deeply, at ease on Chicobi, and in turn, I sensed his ease.

The day after day, the mornings and afternoons, the constancy of care, the work of helping and healing had done more than heal Chicobs of the strangles.

A second event unfolded one year later that finished repairing the crack in the foundational trust of my relationship with Chicobi. My college pal Brenda and I drove north to the camp for a ride. The staff continued to extend my riding rights with Chicobi and even loaned us a second horse. Soon Brenda and I were saddling Chicobi and a camp horse.

With Brenda following, I urged Chicobi down the forest path to the back acres. Soon we walked to the now familiar crest where acres of oak forest sprawled below. It was good to be on Chicobs again. My calves tightened to nudge him down the rock-strewn path and into the forest full of birdsong and blue jay squawks, mossy and musty-wood smells.

I urged Chicobi further into the backlands than we had ever gone. The shade grew deeper. Brenda and I talked boys and then fell silent, enjoying the quiet ride.

Later we were talking of turning campward when we heard something.

Yelps. Panicked yelps. A chorus of panicked yelps.

What? Wolves?

Chicobi's head pointed toward the cries. The yelps were high pitched. Young animals? Distressed? I needed to see. Again my calves pressed Chicobs; he walked toward the sound. The oaks opened slightly into a small clearing. Three tan and black puppies writhed and cried. German shepherds? Here?

Chicobi lowered his head as I dismounted. He nosed the floppy-eared puppies that had scrambled near. The puppies mobbed me, crying, their black eyes desperate. They pushed against each other to touch me. I tried to kneel. They jumped and yelped; their paws scraped my jeans. Brenda dismounted, too, and bent toward the rush of puppies.

Dismay and anger clashed within me. These pups wouldn't have wandered on their own. Not this far. No. "Someone dumped them here, B. Someone left them to die."

We talked. What could we do? We couldn't leave them. But . . . what? Brenda was a novice rider. Could she—what?—hold a puppy and ride? Could I? What would Chicobs do? Would he try to run away with me again?

"We could just lead the horses back and see if they follow." I stood. A puppy clung to me. "Or, B, we could try carrying them." I worried. What if we dropped one? How would the horses act with a squirmy pup on their back? "We have to try."

Brenda agreed. After she settled back into her saddle, I grabbed one of the pups and handed it to her. The pup wiggled—oh no!—

and then went still, its paws on the saddle horn. I handed her the second one that we could take turns carrying.

I threw the reins back over Chicob's head and then scooped up the third pup. It writhed, but I held it firmly before gathering the reins. Chicobi swung his head around. His nostrils moved over the pup who, like his siblings, went still.

What would Chicobs do? Would he even let me mount?

Slightly off-balance, I pushed my boot into the stirrup and hoisted us up. Chicobi stood. The pup remained quiet. It didn't thrash. I pushed my other foot into the stirrup and awkwardly clasped the pup.

We turned the horses homeward and cut through the forest. Chicobi didn't shy or prance. He walked steadily, the camp horse as well, as if they knew our ride had turned into something more.

> *When you are on a great horse, you have the best seat you will ever have.*
>
> WINSTON CHURCHILL

My arm began to burn. I changed hands on reins and pup. "How you doing?" I called over my shoulder.

"Fine!" Brenda was a trouper, which I already knew.

The ride passed slowly, it seemed, and then forest shade lessened and gave way to the open, rocky trail. We were nearing home.

Finally, rocky terrain gave way to meadow, and the boards of the horse pasture appeared. The horses carried us through the meadow, still walking quietly. Ranch hands saw us and stopped their work. Two hurried to us.

"What happened?" A dark-haired staffer reached for the pup. His hand ran over the floppy ears.

"We found them!" I blurted, dismounting to help Brenda. "Someone dumped them. Deep in the backlands."

Others gathered around. Soon, each pup had a new home.

Stretching my arm, I returned to Chicobi and looked into his large eye. All my worry. Gratitude rippled through me. He had understood. He had worked with me. I ran my fingers along his soft muzzle and clasped his neck.

Trust Chicobi? The horse who had sent me into a three-day hospital stay? You bet. The illness. The pups. Our trust had been redeemed.

# Why We Had Ponies

## Lonnie Hull DuPont

W hy did we have ponies?"
I called my older sister, Peggy, to ask her this. I had been talking about the ponies to my husband—a suburbs and city boy who always enjoyed my growing-up-in-nature stories—and he asked me why we had ponies. I had no idea. We had a riding horse—a big palomino gelding named Pal—because my sister loved horses. But even though I'd always been considered the Family Memory, I did not recall why we had ponies. We didn't ride them or enter them in the county fair for prizes or train them to pull a sulky cart . . . or anything else. We simply enjoyed their company.

So why *did* we have ponies? And where did they come from?

Peggy was the true horse lover of the family. She and her horse Pal were best friends throughout her adolescence. He was her 4-H entry at the county fair. She often sat in the barn with him while she did her homework. Pal knew where my sister's bedroom window was, and in the mornings he would whinny to wake her from the fence about twenty yards from the house. My bedroom was next door, and I'd hear Peggy push her wooden window frame up, set aside the screen, and hang over the sill, calling to her big baby Pal.

I remember that our first pony was considered mine, to the extent that we claimed animals. All animals were everybody's at our home. But the cats were more attached to me, the family dog more attached to my parents, and the horses more attached to Peggy. And while I don't recall the details of getting that first pony—a sweet young mare—I do recall that I loved her. Her name was Honey, and her coat was indeed the golden color of honey, and her mane and tail were the color of wheat. I especially loved her blonde eyelashes sweeping over those deep dark eyes. She was fairy tale beautiful.

Now I learned that Peggy knew exactly where our ponies had come from. "Dad brought them home," she said. "Both of them."

Really? It was true that Dad always liked the animals who lived with us. Mom fussed at him for feeding stray cats at the back door. But once in a while, that cat would move in. Dad even built a small swinging door in the wall of his workshop for the cats, something I'd never seen at the time. He was great buddies with the family dog too, and over the years, he was responsible for choosing each subsequent family dog himself.

Though he was quiet about his feelings, it was clear to me that Dad loved our pets. Now that I'm older, I wonder if he perhaps felt unmanly showing it. The midwestern farming mentality where we lived took a more pragmatic view of animals who didn't earn their keep or somehow contribute to the subsistence of humans. Even though my parents' generation no longer farmed the land, that mentality was there.

Bringing home a pony was not quite like bringing home a puppy. But Peggy said a guy at Dad's factory was getting rid of Honey, and Dad brought her home. I forgot to ask how he did that exactly.

Very soon after Honey's arrival, we acquired Lady, a sturdy pony with big patches of dark brown fur on a mostly white body. I don't know who named her, but she had a mature and low-drama way about her, so the name Lady fit her. "Dad brought her home too," Peg said. "A farmer down the road was getting rid of her, and Dad thought she'd be good company for Honey."

So Dad brought home ponies. This was news to me. And I found it delightful to know.

He was really our stepfather, but we called him Dad. He married Mom when I was only five and Peggy was eight, and he did what a good stepfather does—he stepped up to the challenge of raising someone else's children, and he did it the best he knew how. He was a kind man, generous, hardworking, and stoic. In his understated way, he loved Peggy and me—and our dogs and our cats. Neither he nor my mother had any prior horse experience. So it was crazy to learn that he was the one who acquired the ponies. Maybe he simply saw them as larger pets who needed a home.

Honey and Lady became best girlfriends right away, and Pal hovered nearby, a nervous bachelor uncle kept out of the sewing circle, it seemed. Then Lady started gaining tummy weight. A lot. It turned out she had come to us pregnant. Did the farmer know? We sure didn't—for months.

Lady seemed to have the Pregnancy That Would Not End. Many months went by as we sisters sat on the fence in our jeans and cowboy boots and watched Lady, speculating as to when the blessed event would take place. We even started to wonder if maybe she wasn't really pregnant, though her swaying tummy certainly made her look it. We had no knowledge of the almost yearlong gestation period of equines, and there was no internet search to be had then.

Finally early one spring morning I woke to hear Pal whinnying for all he was worth at the fence, trying to rouse Peggy from sleep. I crawled across my bed and looked out my window. I could see movement in the tree line, movement the colors of Lady. She was in there for some reason, and she seemed to have a longer body than she should have. Then I realized she hadn't somehow gotten longer—she'd given birth to a foal with the same coloring as hers. Both momma and baby were in the tree line, maybe to get away from Pal's anxiety.

Peggy was a hard sleeper. I ran into her room and literally shook her awake. "Lady had her baby!"

We threw on clothes and boots and ran outside to the fence to find Lady standing in the tree line with her leggy little foal on the ground. We got close enough to see he was male, and he was chocolate brown with white stockings and a white blaze on his forehead. There was afterbirth around him, caught in the tangle of ground branches.

Mom joined us at the fence. She loved babies of any species, and while Mom cooed over the situation, Peggy was able to negotiate staying home from school to watch the colt get his legs. Hours later when I returned from school, Peggy, Lady, and the colt were in the pasture near the fence, Pal and Honey grazing nearby. The baby was now named Shadow, and he was standing—wobbly but upright.

The sweetest thing was how thrilled Dad was when he got home from work. He should have handed out cigars, that's how pleased and proud he acted. He even drove his elderly mother in from the next town to meet Shadow. I recall her standing at the fence, her pocketbook on her elbow, watching our frisky colt and listening to her son crow about it all. Part of Dad's excitement was that Shadow was born on Dad's birthday, May 2.

From that day on, Dad had a soft spot for Shadow. He liked watching the little guy gallop around. Shadow cocked his head at Dad's voice and then joined him at the fence. Dad had given Shadow's momma a home for her confinement and her delivery, a safe place where she could be part of a stress-free herd. In return, it seemed as if Lady had presented Dad with a birthday gift—her colt.

The day would come when Peggy went off to college. I could not handle the ponies and Pal alone, so Peggy found homes for them all. The pony friends would stay together, and Pal was sold elsewhere. A few years later when Peggy married, she was able to buy him back, and they had a few more years together.

That's all I remember about the ponies. I'm glad I called my sister that day to ask about them. We had a good long talk and some laughter. Then within a few weeks, Peggy died unexpectedly—on May 3, the day after both Dad's and Shadow's birthdays. The conversation about the ponies is the last lengthy one my sister and I had. I'm grateful for that talk and for what we talked about—our shared memories of a childhood full of animals we loved and a kind stepdad who loved them too—and us.

# The Twinkle

## Susy Flory

The first thing you notice when you meet Stetson is how tall he is. In horse talk, he's seventeen hands high. If you stand next to him, you can't see over his back. He's a retired racehorse and he's a big, tall boy.

If you ask politely, he'll bend his head down, and the next thing you'll notice about Stetson is his eyes. They twinkle. Some animals (and some humans) have a dull look about them. It doesn't always mean they're not intelligent. They could be sleepy, or thinking about something else like, *Is it time to eat yet?*

But when you see an inquisitive look directed right at you, paired with a head tilt, a prance, and a graceful tail with a bit of a twitch in it, you know you're in for something of an adventure. And you'd be right.

Some people think horses aren't that smart. Half the time they stand around looking bored. You can usually trick a horse into coming in from their beloved pasture with a handful of hay or a bit of grain in a bucket, then quickly slide their halter on while they munch away. Plus, horses never, ever make it onto those lists of the most intelligent animals. According to scientists, the five smartest animals are chimpanzees, dolphins, orangutans, elephants, and crows.[2] In the area of IQ, even rats and squirrels beat the humble horse.

I knew all this, but looking into Stetson's eyes for the first time made me wonder. When he came into our lives, my daughter Teddy and I were going through a rough patch. I'd been diagnosed with breast cancer in my early forties when she was just fifteen years old. In the end, things had turned out well for me. But the trauma had hit Teddy hard. She'd already been struggling with regular migraine headaches when, in the aftermath of my surgeries and other cancer treatments, a serious infection sidelined her for much of her junior year of high school. We also had my aging mother living with us, which came with its own set of issues. At times, the string of stressful situations was enough to make a preacher cuss, as my dad, a Texas cowboy, used to say.

So Teddy and I decided to find something to do together. Because we both loved animals, and most especially horses, we decided to volunteer at a horse therapy ranch where rescue horses were trained to work with developmentally or physically disabled children. It was a blast, and after a year or so, we fell in love with horses all over again and decided to find one of our own. After an exhaustive online search of approximately thirty minutes, we found a listing for Stetson. He looked beautiful and we liked his name. It had style.

We went to visit, and the owner brought Stetson out on a lead rope. He looked us over out of the corner of his eye and then stretched out that long neck and grabbed the front of Teddy's T-shirt just above her belly button, careful to grab the thin cotton material without nicking her skin. Somehow, she didn't flinch.

When he had her shirt firmly in his front teeth, Stetson pulled her toward him with a gentle but determined tug. She took the cue and let him pull her in, like they were at an old-fashioned dance, then gave him a big hug and fell in love. So did I. We quickly signed on the dotted line.

Of course there were some things to get used to. Stetson was so tall, it felt like sitting on the back of an elephant. The ground was a long ways away, and if I ever fell, or got bucked off, it was going to hurt.

Another problem was his hocks. The joints in the middle of his back legs were a mess. Racehorses are trained hard at a very young age, and their legs often don't develop correctly. Many horses don't survive the track, and those who do often deal with significant arthritis or bone chips that limit their activity or even shorten their lives. Stetson was in this category. We'd have to be careful.

Then there was his training. Somehow, between the eye twinkle and the T-shirt trick, I'd forgotten that he'd had very specific training for a very specific task—to run as fast as he possibly could. In other words, Stetson hadn't been trained to walk or trot gently with a relaxed rider enjoying the scenery on a typical trail ride. He was bred and trained to run.

While we couldn't resist this big beautiful boy, I knew I was going to need professional help to learn how to handle him. Teddy was a natural horse whisperer and felt comfortable on him, even bareback. But I was more nervous; Stetson's training after his racing years were over had been with an English-style saddle and bridle, rather than Western style, which was what I was used to. He'd also had some dressage training, which is like the ballet of the horse world. While Stetson was becoming a healing presence in our lives just by being himself, I knew if I wanted to understand how to better communicate with him, I had a lot to learn.

Our trainer, Denise, had experience training at the Olympic level. I'm not sure how she ended up at the neighborhood barn, but she knew her stuff. Before I started riding lessons, Stetson had already taught me two important things: one, don't pull back on the reins. While that might mean "stop" or "slow down" in Western riding, to a racehorse, it meant "jump forward and take off running as fast as you can." Horse people call this kind of cue a "go button." I learned not to push it. My husband learned the hard way, however, after falling off and breaking his pinkie finger. After that, he was content to watch and cheer us on from the sidelines.

The other lesson Stetson taught me was not to kick his sides. This was really confusing, because in Western-style riding, touching a horse with both heels means speed up. But not with Stetson. He'd stop and then try to turn to one side or another, acting confused. And when he was confused, he'd often start dancing in place like he was about to take off again. Basically he was a giant furry rocket on four hooves just waiting for a chance to practice his running, which he'd been doing his entire life. You couldn't blame him. I was the dumb one in this new partnership.

At my first riding lesson, Denise confirmed what Stetson had already taught me. Then she ran down some other basics: Sit up straight. Rider position and balance are important. Engage your core. Align your heels to your hips and ears. Keep your heels down.

*Okay. That seems pretty straightforward. I think I can do it.*

Over the next few weeks, I tried and listened and learned. Stetson mostly cooperated, and I began to understand that I didn't have to jerk the reins around or kick him in the gut to get him to do something. He could understand very subtle cues. In fact, Denise taught me that when Stetson and I began to get in tune with each other, when I was listening to him with my body and he was listening to me with his body, I could guide him to the left or right with a very light tap of a foot. Later, when I got better, that tap morphed into a light touch of my calf against his side. Next, I learned to turn him by simply looking to the left or the right.

Can you believe it? I could turn a big racehorse simply by turning my head a bit. I couldn't believe it. I still can't.

But it was what she said next that really blew my mind. "Some people think you can tell a horse what to do by just thinking it."

"What? You mean he has some sort of ESP?" I swear Stetson turned his head and looked up at me with his signature twinkle. I patted his withers and smoothed his mane.

"Not exactly," she said. "Instead of turning your head, focus your mind and think about which way you want him to go. But keep your head straight." She stepped back to the side of the arena and nodded.

Here we go. I'm about to try to move a horse with my mind.

I tried it. *Stetson, let's move forward.*

Stetson started walking.

*Now left.*

He turned left, onto the diagonal.

*Now right.*

He did it again. And again. And I have no idea how. I didn't move my head and I'm pretty sure I didn't use any other parts of my body to tell him which way to go. As I practiced, I did find that I had to be clearly focused on him and on which way I wanted him to go. There were times he didn't turn when I wanted him to and I had to use a slight leg squeeze instead. There were days he wasn't that into it, and days I wasn't either. But many times he did get it and did what I asked him to do just by my thinking about it.

I remembered hearing a story from a horse breeder about trying to outwit her horses out in the pasture so she could give them their vaccinations.

"They always run away when I walk into the field with syringes, so I've tried to fool them by putting them in my back pocket where they can't see them," she told me. "I walk slowly toward them, but they know why I'm there and take off to the far side of the field."

One day she decided to try a little experiment, and she slid a couple of screwdrivers into her back pocket instead. They were roughly the same size as the syringes. When she opened the gate and walked across the field, the horses ignored her and stayed in one place. They were relaxed, munching on grass as she walked right up to them. But later, when she switched back and carried syringes in that same pocket (because they still needed their shots) they knew what she had and they bolted.

"I have no idea how they know," she said. "My body language is the same."

I believed her. After many years of being around horses, the breeder knows how sensitive horses are to our moods and the way we hold our bodies, so she's learned to control hers. I've experienced this too. A horse can size you up and read your mood instantly. If you're stressed or irritated from a bad day, your horse is likely to act up and not be easy to handle. If you're sad, they're often sympathetic and ready for a snuggle or a forehead rub. If you're calm and centered, they will be too. Horses are exquisitely attuned to our feelings. But that's not that surprising. Our dogs and cats pick up our feelings too.

But what about detecting the difference between a screwdriver and a syringe in a back pocket? How would a horse know what you're carrying when you're hundreds of feet away? Do they have some sort of X-ray vision? Or how does Stetson know how to go, or turn left or right based on my thoughts? Can he *feel* what I'm thinking? Some sort of equine alchemy, turning thoughts into movement?

Maybe one of these days, horses will climb up the ranks of animal intelligence. But for now, Stetson has taught me to be open to the idea that other living creatures on this earth, especially those not often thought of as smart, might be more intelligent than I thought. Animals just might know far more about what we think and feel than we do about them.

Oh, and if you're ever on a retired racehorse, don't pull back on the reins.

# A Pinto for Pennies

## Jenny Lynn Keller

Asking Santa Claus for a horse and not getting it on Christmas Day just about broke my tender eight-year-old heart. But my younger sister's reaction gained all the attention when the golden-haired tornado threw her usual hissy fit—a polite Southern term for tantrum.

Thank goodness my father quickly salvaged the day and calmed the blue-eyed twister with a creative solution. If my sister and I helped with more household chores the coming year, we would be paid a dollar a week to save toward buying ourselves a horse.

A dollar bill was big money for two young girls back then, and so was every penny we received from other generous sources like grandparents, the Tooth Fairy, and the Easter Bunny. Could we save all our money for twelve long months? Easily we agreed, spit in our palms, and shook hands on the deal. Yeah, I can't believe we used to do that spitting thing either. But what were a few germs among family members, considering some of the other common habits of the day—like not wearing bicycle helmets, seat belts, or bite guards.

By mid-December the following year, my sister and I counted our savings and handed it all to our father. Every coin represented childhood chunks of work and sacrifice—making our beds, folding the laundry, drying the dishes, and shutting our eyes to a huge temptation just a few steps from our front yard. The small country store sitting across the street flashed its "open" sign at us six days a week. A store full of chocolate candy, ice cream, soft drinks, and bubble gum.

Now I ask you, how long can a typical American kid go without any of those life essentials? Barely a week, I'm sorry to say, and these things were the sole reason more pennies than dollar bills filled our piggy banks. Yes, each of us loved chocolate dearly (still do) and owned a large amber glass pig with a money slot on its back and a corked hole in its belly. How much of our hard-earned money resisted temptation and found its way into those piggy banks? My mother carefully recounted the pile of cash spread across our dining table and proclaimed the grand total to be something close to fifty dollars, about half in pennies. My, oh my, were we ever proud of that big sum of money. But was it enough to buy us a horse?

On Christmas morning my sister and I woke up early and raced to look outside the patio door leading to our backyard.

No horse.

"But you promised," we said to our parents.

"Have you seen the big box under the Christmas tree?" they said, pointing into the living room.

We tore into the wrapping paper and found a leather saddle and bridle, well used but nicely polished and smelling exactly like they should—a perfect blend of damp horse hair, hay, and barnyard mud.

"Where's the horse?" my sister said, on the verge of another epic hissy fit.

"Put on your clothes, and we'll show you."

A few minutes later the four of us crossed the street, walked in front of the store, then stopped at the Craftsman-style house beside it. Behind the home was a large field and a barn. My great-aunt and uncle lived in the house, and the field and barn belonged to them.

Guess what we found inside their barn that morning? Surprise, surprise, a white and brown pinto pony, just our size. While other children happily played with their new toys brought by Santa, my sister and I patiently took turns riding our pinto present, Paint.

But this horse story doesn't end on that magical Christmas Day. Many years later I learned the heart-touching truth behind Paint becoming our Christmas pinto.

He was a rescue, in more ways than one. His original owner traveled the country with a carnival company and provided Shetland ponies for its kiddie rides. These ponies were tethered to a large metal wheel, and a quarter would get you a few minutes of going around the circle multiple times. When Paint's owner dissolved his business, he had no need for the ponies. Since they were trained to walk slowly around a circle, the ponies were unsuitable for other purposes.

> *No hour of life is wasted that is spent in the saddle.*
>
> WINSTON CHURCHILL

But Paint suited my father's purpose perfectly. For less than fifty dollars, Paint was delivered to my great-aunt's barn with his saddle, blanket, and bridle. My father bought horse feed with the remaining money and gave his two young daughters a forever memory. Precious pictures are etched in my mind of so many joyful moments as that gentle horse with short legs walked slowly around the barn every evening with us on his back.

When we outgrew Paint, he moved to my grandparents' farm on the other side of town, lived out his years leisurely walking around their barn by himself, then permanently rested in the corner of their back field.

But this story doesn't end there. I didn't know it until this past fall when I spent many hours sitting on the porch with my father and listening to him talk about bygone times. All of us knew he was living his final days on this earth, and he wanted to tell me some things before he died. To my surprise, one of his biggest regrets was a playhouse he never built for me and my sister, another one of the many childhood wants always on our Christmas lists.

When my father apologized for failing to build it, I sat beside him speechless for a few moments as a wave of treasured memories flooded my mind. Cherished remembrances of the idyllic childhood my father and mother gave me and my sister—every year filled with more love, fun, and adventure than many people experience in a lifetime. Had the golden-haired tornado and I ever given that unbuilt playhouse a second thought? Never, and the blue-eyed twister agrees with me. Besides, how many fathers bought their daughters a pinto for pennies?

So I told him the truth. The playhouse didn't matter, the pinto did. As his mind slowly processed my words, he smiled . . . then chuckled.

"I'm glad to hear that," he finally said. "It's been weighing on my heart for years."

Sadly, we didn't have many long conversations like that one before he died. But I am grateful during my father's last days that he knew his kept promise of a Christmas horse meant more to us than anything else on our childhood wish list. And nowadays when I see a horse, I always think about my father and Paint.

During one of those reminiscing moments, I suddenly realized that pinto represented far more than a promise kept and hundreds of rides around the barn years ago. What began as my father's creative solution to buying a horse sprouted seeds of encouragement in two young girls and taught us life lessons continuing to yield positive results even today. Saving my money for Paint years ago initiated a lifelong habit of sacrificing short-term wants for long-term goals. Working those extra household chores taught me that hard work produced rewards. Most importantly, as an extremely shy child, telling others about my horse gave me confidence to talk about other things to more people. Enough confidence eventually to teach corporate and college financial classes.

All because my father bought his daughters a pinto for pennies.

# Flash and Henry

*Rachel Anne Ridge*

My donkey Flash needed a friend.

Now to be clear, in the seven years since we took him in as a stray, Flash had never complained about being alone in our pasture. But I could see it in his posture, his plodding steps, and his deep sighs that he was lonely out there all by himself. At one time he kept company over the fence with the horses that lived in the next pasture, but they'd moved off some time ago. The cows over the other fence, the "B Team" who stepped up as friends when the horses left, had also moved on. Now he was alone. Obviously, he needed a companion—a donkey companion.

I still couldn't believe I was considering acquiring a second donkey for the sake of my *first* donkey's mental state. Never in my dreams would I have imagined I'd be a donkey owner, much less a donkey enthusiast. As a girl, I'd always wished for a horse, a beautiful horse of my own. But since my family lived in the city, owning a horse was never more than a childhood fantasy for me. Much later, when my husband, Tom, and I moved our own family to the country in Texas, I was sure that it was time for my dream to come true.

That was before a stray donkey showed up on our driveway, needing a home. When nobody claimed him, we took him in and named him Flash. It wasn't long before we fell in love with those long ears and gentle expressions of his. His eyes seemed to convey his gratitude, and his big personality began to shine as he became part of our family, which included three children and a dog. To our surprise, Flash the donkey completed our little circle. We loved to pet him, feed him carrots, and let him follow us around the property. He was always curious to see what was going on and could make us smile with his antics and occasional brays.

Now, even the children had moved off to college, and the dog had passed on from old age. Flash was truly alone, and we were concerned. Donkeys are social creatures, designed for life in a herd—or at least with one companion. Lonely donkeys can become lethargic, lose their appetite, or become destructive in their boredom. Flash had taken to stomping on anything we left lying around in the barn, and he seemed to mindlessly wander the pasture as if looking for a friend.

Doc, a burro wrangler at a donkey rescue facility in Texas, had "just the donkey in mind" when I connected with him and told him of our situation. A miniature donkey had just come in with a group of about twenty donkeys from Henderson County, Texas, and he seemed to have a sweet disposition. Doc sent a photo of him, and I immediately fell in love! The tiny chocolate-brown fellow had a cross on his shoulders and a bristly mane that stood straight up. His long fuzzy ears were perked forward inquisitively, and his soft dark eyes seemed to gaze straight into my heart. I was smitten.

Doc told us that he'd been logged into the rescue facility as "Henderson Number Ten," and we thought it made a perfect name for him. We'd call him Henry for short. After a ten-hour round trip to adopt the little donkey, we brought him home and introduced him to Flash.

Flash looked taken aback by the arrival of this stranger. Flash had not seen another donkey since he moved in with us. I knew it would take a few days for the two of them to get used to each other, but I felt confident that they would quickly become best of friends. After all, who couldn't love Flash—the sweetest donkey in the world—and no one could resist Henry, a friendly and calm animal who was eager to be liked. Henry was accustomed to being with other donkeys and would surely show Flash how this companionship thing worked.

Turned out, Henry was just as adorable in real life as I'd imagined him to be from his photo. His gentle disposition was endearing; he was so timid he would only approach me by turning completely around and walking *backward* toward me. His soft eyes and shy attitude invited affection.

At least, that's how he was with *me*.

With Flash, it was another story.

From day one, Henry followed Flash around like a pesky little brother, invading his space. Flash tried to get away whenever he could, but Henry was persistent. He needled Flash, biting and nipping at his legs and neck. One day I watched out the window in horror as Henry jumped up to reach Flash's neck, then chomped down so hard he was able to wheel him around in a circle. Dust went flying all about them as Flash struggled to stay on his feet. Flash let out a high-pitched wheeze and tried to pull back. I could see his confusion as he was brought down to his knees and Henry kicked at him.

I threw open the door and ran to the fence, yelling and clapping my hands to break it up. Only then did Henry let go. He sprang to meet me with a last buck in Flash's direction and then acted as if he was completely innocent, shaking his ears and cocking his head as charmingly as possible.

I was too angry to speak to him. I looked past him to Flash—my beautiful Flash, who nobody better mess with—who appeared dazed.

"Flash, oh Flash! Are you okay?" I reached for the bigger donkey's face as he approached and inspected the bite wounds on his neck. He was bleeding.

Henry stood off to the side and bent forward and scratched his front leg with his teeth as if nothing had happened, which only made me more upset.

"Henry, you cannot do this. You've got to stop!" I lectured him while he simply looked back at me with his soulful brown eyes and blinked.

It's hard to stay mad at someone that cute, but a glance back at poor Flash made it possible. Flash's body language made it clear that he had had enough of this little donkey who had interrupted his peaceful, albeit lonely life.

The weeks passed, and Henry's behavior did not get any better. Out of desperation I messaged Doc, explaining the situation and including a photo of Flash's wounded neck. "Is this normal?" I asked. I was ready to send Henry packing if this kept up.

Doc took a look at the photo. "Yep, that looks pretty awful," his message said, "but don't worry. This is pretty typical behavior while they figure things out. Looks like Flash is going to have to get tough with him."

The last thing I needed was for things to escalate. I was not happy about this at all. I wanted them to figure it out *now*. Even feeding time was a battle I wasn't prepared for.

From the first time I set hay out for them, I knew it was a problem. Henry wanted all of it.

Every bit of it.

He would not let Flash even get close to the hay.

He bucked and kicked his striped little legs at Flash, then raced back and forth between Flash and the hay to keep him away.

Ears back, head down, Flash tried going around him to the left. Henry bucked him back.

Flash tried sneaking past on the right.

Henry put his head down and charged.

Back and forth he dashed, snorting and kicking. His rotund middle, with its light underbelly, swayed with each movement. I stifled a laugh. "Okay, Henry. I know how we can fix this."

I scooped up half the hay and created a separate pile several feet away. Now they could both enjoy their own portions.

Nope.

Henry wanted his pile, and he wanted Flash's pile.

He began running interference on Flash, his portly body surprisingly nimble.

Flash laid his ears back flat and tried to get at one of the piles but was rebuffed again. As dirt flew in all directions, he grunted his displeasure at the determined little donkey.

I stood back and watched the fray over the hay. Henry was so intent on keeping Flash away that he couldn't enjoy a single tasty bite himself.

"Henry, Henry!" I tried to get his attention. "There's plenty for both of you!"

Henry's fixation affected his hearing. There was no talking sense to him.

I set out more hay, more than they could eat in one feeding.

Finally, Henry's hunger won out. He chose the bigger mound and began to eat, pawing at the flake to loosen it. He turned his backside toward Flash to defensively guard his portion, keeping his ears tilted backward so he knew exactly where Flash was every second.

Flash hung back, then tentatively approached the far side of his pile, eyeing Henry. Ears up, alert. He let Henry settle in and begin eating before he started to nibble.

I finally realized I couldn't be upset with Henry. He didn't know why he was frantically reacting this way. In fact, his expression seemed to imply, "Somebody help me! I want to stop kicking, but I just can't!" Unfortunately, all Flash could understand was that feeding time would be a competition.

Both donkeys put on weight over the winter months. The plentiful winter rye grass presented them with a daily feast that they took full advantage of. Flash, with his extra pounds, simply looked bigger and stronger—his appearance enhanced by a bushy cold-weather coat. Henry . . . well, Henry looked like a chubster. His thick winter hair gave him a teddy-bear appearance, which definitely helped me let go of my grudge. Despite my impatience to reach my goals for their relationship, I tried to remain hopeful.

One morning, we awoke to the sight of snow, a rarity in Texas. The landscape was covered in a beautiful blanket of white, with the cedars' boughs in the north woods of the pasture bending low, unaccustomed to the weight. Tom and I donned boots and coats, eager to see what Flash and Henry would make of the snow.

Out of the woods stumbled two groggy donkeys. Henry emerged first, coming to a halt so abruptly that Flash collided right into the back of him—both blinking at the brightness beyond the forest where they'd spent the night. Henry turned to the right and Flash to the left as they took in the scene around them. *What is this stuff?* They sniffed the air, nostrils wide, and they shook their ears as if chasing cobwebs from their heads. We caught their attention, and Flash nudged Henry toward us with surprising gentleness.

With gloved hands, we each took a donkey to scratch as they stopped in front of us: Tom worked on Flash's backside (his favorite spot to get rubbed), while I bent low next to Henry's face. His dark fuzzy ears moved this way and that as he let the morning sun penetrate his thick winter hair. I pressed my lips to his forehead and gave him a kiss. He looked so cute standing in the snow with a confused expression that I found myself clucking over him like a mother hen.

> ### Let's Give a Hand
>
> We note the size of a horse in "hands," and we measure from the horse's withers to the hoof. This goes back to when many things were measured using parts of the ever-convenient human body. A hand to size up a horse was the breadth of a human hand and is now officially four inches or ten centimeters.

"Rachel, look!" Tom whispered. He pointed toward Flash's head.

My heart jumped into my throat. Flash was slowly scratching Henry's back with his teeth. Ever so lightly, he made small biting movements along Henry's dark stripe, as if reassuring him that the snow was nothing to be nervous about.

"He's grooming Henry!" I whispered back, blinking back a tear that formed. It was the first sign that something was changing between them. Henry glanced over his shoulder at the bigger donkey and let out a deep breath, one that signaled complete relaxation. Flash tipped his ears forward and kept up his work along Henry's back.

There, in a snowy pasture under a Texas sky, two donkeys who could never seem to get along took their first real steps toward friendship. One seemed to say, "I see you feel scared." The other said, "Thank you for noticing." It was as if the experience of snow allowed them to put down their defenses and face this new thing together. Maybe it was just enough of a surprise to let them stop competing with one another and simply *be* in the moment. Whatever it was, I felt grateful.

In the coming months I noticed subtle changes. I could see that their fights began to look more like playing. Flash was getting the hang of a donkey activity he didn't even know about before Henry arrived. I watched as they chased each other around the barn and into the covered loafing area to kick up dust and act like brothers wrestling to see who could be first for dinner. It was still too rough for my taste, but Doc's assurance that this is just what donkeys *like* to do helped me stop worrying about it. I began to relax and allow their relationship to take the time it needed to develop.

I wish I could say it was smooth sailing from that time on. But with these two it seemed to be two steps forward and one step back over the eighteen months they had been together. Just when I thought they were over their differences, they'd bicker over a proffered carrot or a handful of grain, and I'd throw my hands up in resignation. Feeding time remained a competition to be first to get the most. Somehow, though, they managed to always stick together. One was never without the other within close proximity in the pasture, and I even noticed that they sometimes lay down next to each other in the barn. Of course, if they realized that I'd seen them dozing just so, they'd jump up and pretend they'd been standing apart the whole time. It was progress—and no matter how small, I'd take it.

One evening, Flash and Henry stood by the fence to supervise Tom and me as we worked in the yard. A high-pitched howl pierced the air, followed by another, then another.

"The coyotes are out early tonight," Tom remarked. We had just finished up some yard work and now paused to listen to the howls and yips that let us know they were around. It was late spring by now, and though we rarely saw them, we knew they had dens nearby.

Now, the coyotes seemed closer to the house than usual. Their howls echoed off the barn and trees, making them sound even spookier than normal. Flash and Henry turned in the direction of the noise. Ears up, nostrils wide, they were on alert that the packs were prowling.

Later we fell asleep to the sound of their howls, glad to be in our beds under the blankets. I didn't think to worry about Flash and Henry.

Flash met me at the gate first thing in the morning. He seemed jumpy and agitated, nervously stomping his feet and nodding his head. He turned and looked toward Henry, who was close behind him. Henry hung back and refused to come near the gate.

Something was wrong.

"Henry! Oh, Henderson Number Ten! What happened, buddy?" I could see from his expression that he was hurt. Opening the gate, I rushed to him, and that's when I saw his ear.

The tip of his left ear was missing.

Bleeding, his raw flesh had been torn in the perfect shape of canine teeth.

"Oh no!" I held his ear and inspected it closely. Razor-sharp teeth marks were all along the jagged edge. My dear little Henry just stared at me with sad eyes, then looked over at Flash.

"Flash, can you tell me what happened?" How I wished he could explain everything. Hands shaking, I began to inspect both donkeys for injuries. Henry had deep scratches on his forelegs and on the back of his back leg. Flash had bloody marks on his legs and face.

There had obviously been a violent scuffle.

Coyotes.

Henry, small enough to be preyed upon, had been attacked in the middle of the night. I could only imagine how scary it must have been. Flash now nudged Henry, who looked as if he'd just survived the worst night of his life. Flash must have saved him! It was the only explanation. I put my arms around Henry and realized how easily he could have been killed, had Flash not been there. Thank God they only got an ear.

Flash bent his head over Henry as if to say, "I'm here for you, buddy." Henry made a whimpering sound and gazed back in gratitude. Ears forward, eyes closed, their noses touched.

These two had come so far, and my heart melted into a puddle.

Friendship takes time. How had I missed this simple fact? I'd started with such unreal expectations of these two donkeys: I assumed that all I had to do was put two donkeys into a pasture together, and they'd get along instantly. I brought Henry home so he would support Flash and meet his needs, and I thought this arrangement would create an immediate bond between them. I wasn't prepared for Henry having his own ideas about things, or Flash having to learn what it means to even *be* a donkey. I didn't take into account their independent streaks, or their competitiveness, or their need to build trust with each other. These donkeys reminded me that relationships develop through shared experiences and common ground. A friendship can't be rushed, and sometimes it takes nearly losing it to realize just how precious it really is. Perhaps Flash and Henry knew the secret all along: friendship arrives on its own terms, and simply being there for each other is one of life's greatest gifts.

# Black Giant

## Karen Lynn Nolan

From my earliest memories, I fantasized about having a horse of my own. Even though I grew up in Kentucky, famous for its horses, I seldom saw one. They were rare in the mountains where my family lived. When Daddy took us to visit my grandmother, though, I glimpsed a muddy and unkempt horse fenced into a minute patch of grass on a hillside. I yearned to rescue him, bathe away the mud and dirt, and brush his matted russet-colored hair until it glistened in the sun like my imaginings of my favorite literary horse—Black Beauty. Mom had splurged to purchase the book for me when I was three and used it to teach me to read. I soon fell in love with the book and the story. Oh, to have my own horse to love.

One early spring morning, while the fickle weather debated between winter and spring and fog still lay heavy in the hollers, I met my first horse. Daddy rose earlier than usual that morning and headed outside. I followed, as I usually did, eager to spend time with him on his day off. He dragged a new metal contraption out of his storage shed.

With a wag of his finger he spoke in his mountain drawl. "Stand back, Karen Lynn, this thing could hurt you."

I obeyed and watched him from a safe distance as he fitted all the pieces together and dragged the finished project to the bottom of the hill behind our house. His face glowed red, and sweat dripped from his chin. His white tank undershirt bore the stains of sweat as he removed his flannel shirt and hung it over a lower limb of the locust tree.

"Karen, you stay away from that plow while I'm gone. You hear me? It's sharp and could cut you up." He wagged his finger at me again.

"Where you goin', Daddy? Can I come with you?" I loved taking little trips with my daddy.

"No. Not this time." He turned to walk toward the road.

"Why not? Please?" I pouted.

"I have to walk to get it and I can't take care of you and it at the same time. Go inside with your mother while I'm gone."

The screen door slammed behind me as I marched past Mommy and out to the front porch to watch where Daddy would go. It didn't take long for him to disappear down the road. I sat in the swing and waited. Curiosity had me guessing what the "it" could be.

After what I reckoned was an eternity, I caught sight of him coming back down the road—leading a horse. I squealed and ran to the end of the driveway to wait for them. My little heart nearly burst with anticipation. The horse was black, but not sleek and shiny like Black Beauty. I didn't care. It was a horse.

Daddy yelled to me as they approached, "Get back. You might scare him so's he'd bite or kick ya."

I backed up against the hedge bushes, giving the horse plenty of room to pass. It hadn't dawned on me I should be afraid of him until then. I cautiously followed them to the back of the house, where Daddy had left the plow.

"Is he ours, Daddy?" I squeezed my hands together and flattened my back against the side of the house.

"No, honey, he's just here to plow the garden." Daddy led the horse to the front of the plow he'd built earlier and started hooking it up to him.

The bit in his mouth reminded me of how much Black Beauty hated his. Poor horse.

"What's his name?" The horse towered above Daddy. I never realized they were so big.

"Don't reckon it's got none." He kept hooking things together.

"I'll call him . . . Black Giant. That's a good name, ain't it?"

Daddy paused a moment and looked at me with his blue-gray eyes. "That's a fine name, Karen Lynn."

Daddy led Black Giant up to the apple tree and lined him up with the bottom edge of the garden. He straightened the plow behind Black Giant, clicked his tongue, and tugged on the reins. Black Giant knew exactly what to do. He snorted, nodded his head, and plodded across the mountainside in a perfectly straight line. When they reached the end, Daddy told him, "Whoa." He did. Then they turned and headed back across.

I sat on a tree stump below the first plowline and watched Black Giant work. Back and forth he trudged on the side of the mountain, pitting straight lines into the hardened earth. Daddy seemed small behind him as they worked.

Black Giant wasn't sleek, shiny, and well-tended like Black Beauty. His body was sturdy, hardworking black. He didn't prance or gallop, he clomped. He reminded me of me. I, too, exhibited the characteristics of a mountain workhorse, stout and ungraceful, instead of a sleek and graceful thoroughbred.

When Daddy and Black Giant had worked their way up the side of the hill to the fence around an old cemetery, Daddy led him back down. "Easy, easy, boy." The plow and chains chinked with each step. At the bottom, Black Giant whinnied and snorted as

Daddy removed his gear. Black Giant seemed to enjoy the work more than standing around.

I eased up close enough to smell him. My nose wrinkled. He needed a bath. I craned my neck to gaze into his dark eyes. If only I could touch him. If only I could explain to him how I admired him and his hard work, so we could plant our garden and have food to eat. Daddy probably appreciated him too. The year before, our first year at this house, Daddy had plowed the garden himself, using a pitchfork. It took a long time. Much longer than Black Giant took.

Thoughts of the beans, corn, tomatoes, okra, peppers, onions, chard, and much more that would fill our table for summer encouraged my tummy to rumble. After the growing season, Mom and Daddy would can the leftover food so we could eat from the garden all winter.

I smiled into Black Giant's eyes rimmed by long eyelashes. He turned his head toward me and whinnied. How I wished I could speak horse. I wanted to touch his nose. Run my fingers through his tangled mane.

"Daddy, can I touch him? Please?" I squeezed my hands together and begged.

Daddy sighed a Daddy sigh and wiped sweat from his forehead. "I'll have to hold you."

I practically jumped into Daddy's sweaty arms. He moved close to Black Giant's head. I leaned forward and stroked his nose. He didn't seem to mind at all. I ran my fingers down the dusty hairs of his mane.

"You're beautiful, Black Giant. Thank you for coming today."

"I need to take him back now." Daddy put me down. "Stand back so he doesn't step on you." Daddy took his reins and clicked with his tongue to tell Black Giant to come with him.

"Is he ever going to come back again?"

"Yep. He'll be back after all the food's gone this fall."

"Yay." I squealed and did a little barefoot dance in the grass.

I watched them walk down the driveway toward the main road. A breeze blew down the mountainside and brought with it the fragrance of freshly tilled earth and horsey odors. A tear leaked from the corner of my eye as I followed them to the end of the driveway. Daddy led Black Giant down the road and back to his owner on the other side of the hill. If only he could stay. I sighed. At least he would return. I knew we could become great friends.

Black Giant returned to our hillside every spring and fall for several years. I'm certain he recognized me as he whinnied and turned to me so I could stroke his nose. As I grew taller and braver, our friendship grew too. He seemed to look forward to our moments together. Perhaps it was because I was the only one who stroked his nose and spoke kindly to him. We seemed to need each other.

The day came when Black Giant didn't return. Daddy never told me why. I still think of him and smile. My Black Giant, my horse, my friend.

# Not According to Plans

## Nicole M. Miller

I never really thought I had a shot.

I was seventeen and life was busy: high school, working in my spare time at a barn, showing my horse, nighttime college classes for extra college credits, and university campus tours each weekend. In the midst of it all, my friend convinced me to try out for the local county fair court—a trio of hair-spray laden teen girls bedazzled in sequins, glitter, and fringe tasked with traveling to other fairs and rodeos as ambassadors.

It sounded fun. I was the horse-obsessed girl who was also a bit type A. On top of my National Honor Society membership, drama club role, and half a dozen other extracurricular activities, I thought this would look good on my resume and college applications.

But I wasn't the blonde pageant-girl cutout. I was a dark-haired nerd and on the bigger-boned end of the teen girl spectrum. Still, I wrote the speech, practiced a predetermined riding pattern on horseback, and studied horse and rodeo trivia.

I'd spent a half dozen years in equestrian 4-H attending the county fair that I was hoping to represent. More than anything, I poured myself into practicing the riding pattern that involved a series of speed changes, quick stops, and spins.

I had a particular knack for flubbing up patterns by forgetting one tiny detail in the moment, and it had cost me a championship ribbon one year. (Seriously, the judge walked up to me after the class and told me if I hadn't forgotten that one piece of the sequence I would have won it all. Instead, I didn't even make it into the top five.)

We paid to board my horse at a nearby stable so I could ride in a covered arena.

Day after day.

Pattern, speech (delivered from horseback after the pattern), study.

Repeat.

The more I practiced, the more I thought I might really have a shot. I might not have the "look," but maybe if I had the riding chops and speech down . . .

The day of the tryouts arrived, and I'd worked harder to prepare for this than almost anything I'd ever done. My friend and I curled our hair, applied hair spray, pressed our outfits to perfection, and solicited help from a bona fide Mary Kay consultant.

We looked goooood.

Next we drove to the barn to get our horses. The barn manager walked up to me before I'd even stepped from the truck.

"Hey, Nikki," she said, holding her hands out in a calming motion. "Now, Zip is okay, but he seems to have come down with the flu."

All my carefully laid plans came screeching to a halt and slamming into each other like the cars of a derailed train.

If my horse had the flu, there was no way I could take him to the tryouts.

I closed my eyes. *Don't cry. Don't cry. You can't mess up your makeup!*

Yes, vain, I know, to worry about my makeup at a time like that.

My mom and my friend's mom swirled about as if to quell my panic, but contrary to my typical emotional responses, I felt calm. My aunt, who had lent me her horse, Zip, to ride for the tryouts and beyond if I made the court, went to look after the horse.

The clock was ticking. We'd be late if we didn't leave soon, and my friend (with her perfectly healthy horse) was anxious to load up and get to the tryouts arena.

The barn manager spoke above the buzz. "You could take Joe!"

*Joe?*

She led us to a pasture and pointed to a sway-backed gelding who I think was chestnut colored, but through the three-inch layer of mud and caked-on manure, it was impossible to tell.

"Yeah, he's broke to ride! Dead quiet under saddle."

Done! We had no other option. My mom and aunt loaded Joe and me into the truck and trailer and we were off.

I'd never even noticed Joe in the pasture before, and I hadn't had a lot of experience riding horses I'd never even met in a competition. But the pageant wouldn't wait for us, and there were seven girls competing for three coveted spots.

My mom and aunt dropped my friend and me off at the building for the interviews and raced off to clean up Joe in time for the riding portion, in an hour or so.

I moved in a haze and went through the motions we'd practiced—I dressed in a fancy western-style dress, sat with the three judges, and joked and laughed about the insanity of the day. After the personal interviews, each contestant did a series of impromptu questions on the stage in front of a crowd, and all my nerves gave way to the realization that the whole pageant was entirely beyond my control. So I just answered everything as me: no pretense, no false bravado. The judges seemed to like it.

We moved from the interviews down to the riding arena, changed into starched and pressed Wrangler jeans, and secured our cowboy hats with duct tape and bobby pins. (Not kidding on this one—if your hat falls off in the arena, it's frowned upon. Many, many headaches were and are endured by rodeo royalty for the sake of well-secured hats.)

I then learned how thoroughly entrenched the mud and grime were in old Joe's fur. My aunt and mother were both splattered with water as they'd tried to get the horse clean, but they simply didn't have the time. They cleared out a spot for the saddle and girth and had to call it good. The judges were informed of my sick horse and granted me a pass on this lapse—horse cleanliness and presentation were part of the overall score.

We were given a short time to warm up our horses, and the judges allowed me an extra ten minutes since I'd never ridden Joe before.

Good old Joe. The twenty-five-year-old, "dead broke" horse. I tried to urge him into a canter (one of the key speeds for the pattern) and lo and behold . . . he started bucking. Perhaps he thought we were trying out for a different role within the rodeo community—like the bucking broncs or something. I kept my balance and struggled to keep my composure.

Forget doing the pattern well—I just needed to survive. I settled him down and took him through the paces again. He'd throw in a little buck every now and then. And then I ran out of warm-up time. I rolled my shoulders back, lifted my chin, and took a deep breath.

When the gate opened, I pulled out every skill and trick I had from six years of riding to control the horse. Joe kept his bucking to a minimum during the pattern, and I hit about every cue and exercise throughout the pattern. At the end of the pattern, my heart raced, and they handed me the wireless microphone to deliver my speech.

Joe managed not to buck during the speech, though he refused to stand still. I stumbled a bit through the speech as I wrestled with the reins to try to get him to settle. Somehow we finished, and I couldn't have been happier to leave that arena.

I'd made it. I was fairly certain that the disaster of a ride would mean I lost a spot in the top three, but I knew it was out of my hands.

Still. God had provided me a horse when mine fell ill. I was able to take the chance to do what I'd spent months preparing for. And I'd done my very best.

After an hour of the judges tabulating scores and deliberating, the seven contestants and their friends and families gathered in the small event center and waited for the results. Like teen girls at the tense climax of a chick flick, we seven contestants stood on stage with nervous smiles.

The first princess was named, a beautiful blonde. The next was my friend, who'd walked with me every step of the way. I was thrilled for them both. And I was wholly unprepared for the next moment.

I was named as the final princess.

Afterward, one of the judges approached me. "Honey, you are the best rider I've seen in years. I can't believe you did so well on a horse you'd never even ridden before. I'd like to talk to you about doing more pageants in the future."

That ride, on that horse I hardly even remember to this day, set me on a path of discovery: of my abilities, my strength, my resilience, my joy in public speaking, and my heart for community service. It also helped me break through the pretense of what I thought the judges would want to see and encouraged me to simply be myself.

Never again was I nervous about riding a horse I didn't know. In fact, I relished every chance I found to ride a new horse to test my skills further.

This led me to try out for another title—the teen title to represent every rodeo in the state. It was a grueling seven-day pageant where the horsemanship horses were selected at random, and my confidence came through as I was given one of the most difficult horses and yet still was awarded the horsemanship category. To date, this is one of my proudest accomplishments.

Oh, and did I happen to mention that a guy friend of a friend at that county tryout just so happened to be intrigued by that dark-haired girl on the ugly bucking horse? That fellow would later call me up and ask me out.

After five years of dating, we got married. We now have two boys, two dogs, and two horses. If God hadn't provided old Joe, I never would have taken part in the tryouts, and I would not have met my future husband.

I learned through Joe that, while things don't always happen according to your plans, God has a hand in it all. He provided me more through that ornery mud-covered horse than I ever would have attained with a perfect, bump-free ride.

From then on, I embraced the changes and twists in the road as they came. I look for the times when I can choose the horse I've never ridden. Then I hold on tight, knowing God's got an even bigger, better thing in mind.

# A Horse Called Lady

## Sandy Cathcart

I always believed a horse called Lady was my special healing balm. It wasn't until recently I realized she was also my father's healing agent. In fact, she did more for my father and me than any human could ever do.

It all began back in first grade at Camp Pendleton, California. I was proud of my father, the Marine, even at that young age. The general's son was in my class, and all the other students and even the teacher treated him as if he was something special, following him around during recess and doing whatever he wanted to do. Not me! I played by myself in a corner of the schoolyard, believing my dad was every bit as good as the general.

Dad was very proud of being a Marine. He would often say, "You can take the man out of the Marines, but you can't take the Marines out of the man." To this day I can still sing every word of the "Marine's Hymn."

I was still a little girl when the United States went to war with North Korea, and Dad was due to ship out with his unit. Momma spent a lot of time crying for fear Dad would be killed, but Dad wanted to serve his country in just such a way. "I'm doing this for Sandra," he said, "and for all the other children, so they can have a future." It was his belief that if we didn't stop the war on the other side of the world, it could come to our doorstep.

The day before Dad was to ship out to Korea, he suddenly fell ill and ended up in the hospital with severe bleeding ulcers. For weeks, he convalesced until he was finally discharged from both the hospital and the Marines. Broken in spirit and body, Dad loaded up our car with our few possessions, and we traveled to Northern California near the Trinity Mountains. It was there we were starting over on a 1,500-acre ranch. And it was there that a horse called Lady helped him heal.

Lady was an unwanted horse. I don't know if she had been mistreated or if she simply had an enormous stubborn streak. Not even the toughest cowboy in Scott Valley could break her. One day Dad and I were at a small auction where all the cowboys had gathered when Lady was brought into the arena. We heard people whispering that no one would buy her. "She's sure to end up in a glue factory," one cowboy said.

"Dad," I said, pulling on his shirt. "Is that true? Will Lady be killed?"

Dad shook his head. "Don't know, Sandra. Strange world we live in."

I knew Dad wanted a horse. He had told me many stories about how he grew up in Oklahoma and how he rode horses with his cousins. His father, John Speed Taylor, was a US marshal, and when Dad was only three years old, my grandfather put Dad in the saddle with him while he transported prisoners across state lines. Dad said it was a frightening thing to be sitting around campfires at night worrying if prisoners would try to escape. But none ever did, and Dad's memories always centered on the horse.

So on this day, when I heard that Lady might go to the glue factory, I began wishing with everything in me that Dad could save her. I didn't realize until later that my wishing was really a prayer and that I could ask God to answer just such a prayer.

Lady's reputation had grown far and wide throughout our little valley. We watched as a cowpoke tried to put a saddle on her back. He barely got out of the way as she began bucking and kicking, snorting and wheezing, and all before any human touched her back. And when they did, they were off as fast as they were on. That is, until my father walked over to her.

I don't know what words he spoke to Lady while we all watched from a safe distance, but I swelled with pride when Lady stood still and lowered her head to my dad's chest. When her tail began to swish, Dad set the bit into her mouth and raised the reins over her head. She barely twitched. Forgoing a saddle, Dad ran a hand across her back and hopped on.

Not one cowboy let out so much as a whisper as Lady walked around that corral with Dad on her back. It was as if she had been born for just such a moment. Dad leaned over and whispered into her ear before climbing down and leading her to a sawhorse where a saddle lay waiting. She quivered some when he set the saddle on her, and she turned her head as if for reassurance. It was so quiet we could hear Dad tell her what a good girl she was. Then Dad climbed in the saddle and sat proud and tall as Lady began her procession. This time the crowd went wild, and Dad picked up the pace. I've never seen anything so beautiful as Dad on that horse, but what he did next surprised everyone.

He led Lady over to the place where I was standing on the other side of the fence. I was seven years old at the time, just a young whippersnapper, as Dad often noted. I still remember the smell of dust as Lady walked around that corral. "Come on up, Sandra," Dad said. "Do it slow and easy."

The crowd gasped in unison, and someone yelled out that Dad was nuts. But I had no fear. I was never afraid when Dad told me to do something like that. He had taught me that animals will trust you if you aren't afraid, and I had seen that to be true many times on our ranch. Taking my dog Nipper with me, I roamed through the forest without a care in the world. Once I talked to a coyote, sure that he could understand every word I said.

I crawled through the rails of the fence and made my way to Lady. Like my father, I spoke soft words to her, telling her how beautiful she was and thanking her for giving us a ride. Her ears turned toward me and her soft nose nuzzled my hair. I ran my fingers over the softness of her nose before lifting my hands to my father. He pulled me up in front of him. It was the first time I had ever sat on a horse, and my heart was immediately stolen.

Lady walked us around that arena like it was a Sunday go-to-meeting day. At the end, Dad pulled to the fence away from the crowd and had me climb off Lady and onto the rail, then he climbed off and led her back to her handler.

Once the handler took hold of the reins, Lady became a bucking bronco. The man cursed as he tried to get her under control. Her eyes were wild with fright and she turned back to my father, pleading with him to save her.

"Good for nothing animal!" the man yelled. Then he threw the reins toward my father. "You can have her. Give me fifty bucks, and she's yours."

Fifty bucks was a lot of money for us back in those days. Dad had to shake his head. "Don't have it," he said, handing back the reins.

But then a strange thing happened. Money began flying into the corral, and we left that day with Lady as our horse.

Dad and I continued to be the only ones who could ride her. Once my grandfather tossed me up on her, and she bucked me right back into his arms. From then on, I climbed on by myself. There were plenty of fences where I could get up to her height.

Being an only child and living on a remote ranch would have proved unbearably lonesome for me if it weren't for my dog Nipper and our horse called Lady. Lady gave me companionship and made me feel special by allowing me to ride. I spent many summer afternoons telling her all my troubles.

Her healing for Dad went much deeper. When we first moved to the ranch, Dad was strangely quiet and easily angered. I didn't understand at the time how much he had lost. We had moved from a busy city to a remote ranch. He had lost his strength and his identity as a Marine, of which he was always proud. Working with Lady, his strength soon returned and his identity in the community as the only cowboy who could ride her gave him back his pride. He became less angry and more like the father I had known in Camp Pendleton, the father who believed he could do anything if he set his mind to it.

Lady herself received healing as well. By the time we had to move from our remote ranch and back to the city, we worried what to do with Lady. One day, Dad was talking with our neighbor, who had just lost his wife to cancer. Lady began nuzzling the man's chest, and the two immediately fell in love. She seemed to understand he needed her as much as we had. Dad left Lady with our neighbor that day, and we all ended up in tears.

I will always be grateful to God for giving my dad and me a horse called Lady. She gave us something no human could ever give—a sense of belonging and purpose and an identity that can never be stolen.

# Shiloh in the Mist

## Connie Webster

I've loved horses all of my life but was not able to have one for a long time. I got my first horses as a novice at the age of forty-four. The person who sold the horses to me knew that I was unknowledgeable, actually clueless. She had two horses available on her farm that she said would work for me. They would have been good horses for someone who had some horse experience, though I would eventually realize they were not a wise choice for a first-time horse owner like me.

I wasn't planning to buy two horses, but I did. Maggie was a beautiful black gaited mare. Wilma was an aged Tennessee Walker, chestnut with a flaxen mane and tail. I was so excited and full of hopes for my life with these two horses. But once I got them home, I wasn't sure of the next step.

I walked into the pasture with a halter and lead rope to get to know them. As I neared the horses, they moved just far enough away to be out of reach. I continued on my quest with lead and halter in hand for sometimes hours at a time and with little or no success. Those first weeks I would eventually walk back to the house feeling frustrated and hopeless.

This was before the age of computers and Google and online searches, so I purchased several books to read and asked questions of those who had any horse knowledge. I kept trying, failing, then trying again and again, thinking, *Maybe this will help me get closer to my horses.* Anything new I read I wanted to apply to my horses and my relationship with them, as this was my first love. I wanted so desperately to fulfill the dream of my little girl heart.

As providence would have it, I ran into Sharry, a high school friend, one day in the grocery store. She had had horses almost all of her life, and we began talking about them. Sharry encouraged me to continue to work toward my heart's desire. She told me that she was going to sell one of her horses, and she wanted to give me the opportunity to experience a truly well-trained horse. This mare was much older, a quarter horse/Arabian cross. She had been used extensively by my friend and her daughter over the years in a variety of disciplines at the local county fair as well as being ridden as a trail horse. Her daughter now had a flashy show mare, so they wanted this mare to go to someone who would love and care for her for the rest of her days.

When I first met and rode Shiloh, I realized that indeed she would be the perfect horse for me. She was quiet and steady and willing to go anywhere I asked her to go. She took such good care of me as well as my young daughters, who rode her on occasion.

As far as looks went, she was pigeon-toed and ewe-necked. She had the large head of a quarter horse but the petite body of her Arabian bloodline. Her coat was what is referred to as "flea-bitten"—creamy white with tiny dark specks. Her conformation was poor, and she would have been considered homely by many. But because of her incredible heart and her willingness to do anything I asked, she was the most beautiful horse I had ever known.

I found good homes for Maggie and Wilma. Now through Shiloh I was able to live my childhood dream of having a horse I could care for and love. I could walk her out and saddle up and ride anywhere at any time without worries. She was truly worth her weight in gold. There was a lovely lane out back between two cornfields. Shiloh and I would ride along in the morning sun. I would sing the song from *Oklahoma* "Oh, What a Beautiful Mornin'" at the top of my voice. Such happy memories.

As a young girl I read many horse books, one of which was *A Horse in the Mist*. It was a story of a young girl who sees a white horse standing in her backyard on a moonlit night. Could it be a ghost? When she goes out in the morning, it is nowhere to be found, but of course the story ends with the girl finally catching her lovely horse. Since no one else cares to keep the horse, she is able to claim it as her own. A predictable but happy ending. As I watched Shiloh out in the paddock on summer nights, she reminded me of that story. My own horse in the mist.

I knew Shiloh was older, and she began to show her age. She was having a hard time keeping her weight, and she would drop food from her mouth as she ate, so I took her to an equine dentist who could correct her bite and help her to get the nutrients from her feed. As he worked on her, he told me that he had never seen a horse so old. By the wear of her teeth he guessed her age to be thirty-six, though she looked younger due to the care I had given her through the years. He told me to keep up the good work and continue feeding as I had.

We enjoyed several years together, but time eventually took its toll and Shiloh became too frail to ride, though she was still a joy to have and care for. It became hard to keep weight on her, and she began to struggle to keep warm through the long winters. So I blanketed her on the cold days and warmed her senior feed and water. I could tell she appreciated all the love and care she received. She talked to me each time she saw me heading her way in the morning and would always come to meet me in the pasture. She was my heart horse, my sweet mare.

The time eventually came to say good-bye for the sake of my beloved Shiloh's comfort. It was May, that lovely month in spring that is full of the promise of warmth and beauty and of the coming summer. I got Shiloh through that last winter, but she was not picking up weight as she had in the years before once the cold weather was past. She began to have episodes of colic, and then my vet discovered she had cancer.

So I showed her that last act of love, which was so very, very hard. She is buried out by my barn, beside a beloved dog. My daughter gave me the gift of a crab apple tree to mark her grave. Shiloh no longer resides in my barn, but her memory lives on. Sometimes on the summer evenings when the sky is clear and the moon is shining down, I picture her there in the paddock, enjoying her quiet spot.

# My Horse Coworkers

## DJ Perry

*T*he glorious Persian stallion raced across the white beach—each thunderous hoof kicking up a spray of water and sand from the ocean's edge . . .

Many children grew up reading literature like this—admiring such notable horses as Seabiscuit, Shadowfax, Trigger, and My Pretty Pony, all part of a rich mythology full of famous horses. Reader imaginations were fed by a steady diet of heroic horsey deeds that stole hearts in adoration of these magnificent animals.

Growing up, I too enjoyed such tales of flying horses with Greek heroes astride them, ready to battle wicked monsters. But the average, standard variety horse minus wings or magic horn never quite enchanted me.

To many, horses inspired a deep love, a feeling that their soul was intertwined with the spirit of the horse. I just happen to *not* be one of those people. No special spirit/animal connection for me—just a respect. Don't get me wrong, I don't have any issues with my horse amigos. I'm just a dog person. I could rattle off a long list of dogs versus horses comparative bullet points, but let's just leave it that dogs are much cheaper to feed.

That said, I've worked with many horses during my course of employment as an actor for TV and film. But they were more like coworkers, and, much like fellow human employees, various personalities exist. Let's take a look at a few of my horse coworkers.

I was starring in a short Western film being shot at a small logging town built behind a large plantation house in Virginia. The original family that lived in the house rested behind a wrought-iron fence in a small 1800s graveyard. I was playing the Oklahoma Kid, and my horse was named Ned, as I recall. Ned was not a handsome horse and not overly young or athletic. I remember how tired he looked the first time I met him, like one of those zombie coworkers who gather around the coffeepot trying to jump-start their morning. Hiring the best horse costar must have been a lower priority on the production list.

I imagined Ned was one of those horses you see at the county fair, walking in a circle with young children bouncing on his back. One day Ned probably just refused to walk in a circle anymore and was sent off to a retirement farm. He probably stood in a nice pasture for a good long time until someone desperately in need of a film horse remembered ole Ned.

I met Ned with all the respect I give any of my human costars. He awoke slightly to my voice and nose rub. Upon seeing nothing food-like before him, Ned's eyes closed again. And after that, I heard a snore. A horse snoring. I'll be. I didn't know horses could do that.

The second assistant director (in charge of talent) approached and seemed happy to see our apparent bonding. He told me that in this shot, we'd go to the far end of the field and run hard toward camera, staying as close to camera left as possible.

The AD walked off. I looked at Ned to see if he was paying attention to our instructions. It did not seem like he was. But at least he stopped snoring when I climbed on his back. Was Ned part of the noble line of horses brought to America by the Spanish or descended from the lines of historical heroic horses? Questionable.

I walked Ned to the far end of the field. Whatever the tripod-mounted camera looked like in the wheat field, it definitely did not look like anything Ned wanted to get close to. Waking Ned up and getting him to move faster than a walk to the end of the field was a task in itself. I could swear he was walking with his eyes closed. I might even have heard another snore.

*Action!* I kicked Ned off, and he was running toward the camera when suddenly he pulled hard right. *Cut! Reset. Back to one.* We were rolling film, not digital, and multiple takes cost money.

*Take 2—action.* Ned pulled hard left, way in advance of the camera, which was burning through film stock. Ned kept moving out of frame, to the dismay of our director. He apparently didn't know what that thing pointed at him was, but he was not going to ride close to it. I tried everything I knew to do, but . . . nope. Okay. We got enough before Ned ran out of frame. *New set up.*

Did we get what production needed? I was told we would just cut out early to the shot of Oklahoma Kid riding up to the hitching post. We walked to our first position mark in the new scene, our starting point. I was ready. Ned was asleep.

*Wake up, Ned! Action!* I got Ned to trot up to the hitching post. I started to get off, and he decided to turn around and walk off. I think a patch of wildflowers caught his attention. *Cut! Back to one.*

We reset, and now at least Ned was awake with a mouthful of clover and ready. *Action!* I rode up just like John Wayne. Good dismount. I wrapped the reins and started to walk off. Ned decided to follow and pulled the Cherokee fence right down—dragging it. *Cut! Cut! Cut!*

Another couple of takes and we finally got our shot. Was Ned untrained in the tasks? Maybe. Or maybe he just felt this wasn't in his job description.

Another coworker was a young, lean black horse named Diablo's Child, or DC as I liked to call him. With a name like that, any God-fearing person should have considered themselves warned. Unlike Ned, this horse was full of energy and alert to everything going on around him. But someone must have failed to read the small print on DC's resume that read "Dislikes snakes."

Anyone knowing the serpent's role in the Garden of Eden story might get a chuckle from that last bit. I also am not a fan of snakes on the whole. I mean, especially the ones with the venom sacks on the sides of their wide heads. So, much like my coworker DC, I too avoid them as a rule of thumb.

We were shooting a visual synopsis—a story pitch for a Western film. It's meant to build hype and sell investors. I was playing the frontier father, and the scene was a classic cowboy speech given just before the hero sets off to save the day. This seemed like it would be an easy go. DC was alert, active, and taking rider direction on point.

The reins placed against one side of DC's neck caused him to turn. A slight kick with my heels moved us to a trot, another kick to a gallop, and lastly a run.

Since we were filming around this 1800s cabin with lights, audio, and cameras, the crew had black cables running throughout this area. DC and I were brought into the middle of the cabin's yard so the crew could look at our placement for lighting, sound, and composition. I sat proudly atop DC, watching all this activity, feeling happy with how smooth and uneventful our shoot day was unfolding.

The director of photography (in charge of capturing the front of camera action) called for a lighting change. Our industrious crew started moving lights around, and I noticed a jolt go through DC. It was as if he had urinated on an electric fence. I saw that his eyes, partially covered with blinders, were huge like saucers.

As a concerned coworker, I asked DC if everything was okay. A slithering sound caught my attention. I saw that the electric team was pulling cables through the grass. It looked like snakes everywhere, moving quickly, surrounding us.

I felt DC's body tense up and his panic attack coming. I don't really recall what happened next. Lucky for us, we had footage of it from a behind-the-scenes camera. I remember pondering if I had time to dismount. Before I could formulate an answer, I found myself balancing on the back of a straight-up bucking bronco.

Martial arts training and some horsemanship—but mostly fear of getting dropped on my head and being confined to a wheelchair—resulted in me riding Diablo's Child. Not just for eight seconds. I rode him until he calmed down. When we watched the footage, I understood why not one person on that crew thought I would stay on that horse's back. DC had a dislike for snakes, but I have a dislike for being thrown from horseback.

Now, I don't want to be one of those people who only talk poorly of their coworkers. We all have a few of those types around us in the workplace. But let's not forget our professional, outstanding coworkers who do their job perfectly.

On another Western in Arizona, I found myself working opposite a few actors I hold in high regard—Mr. David Carradine, maybe best known for his *Kung Fu* TV series and *Kill Bill*, and Wes Studi, a Native American actor from two of my favorite period pieces, *Dances with Wolves* and *Last of the Mohicans*.

I've had amazing horse coworkers too. One set, I was instructed to ride up hard with my horse and give warning to another rancher about trespassing. Just before *Action*, my stirrup broke under my foot. I think my horse's name was Cloud, and he floated just like one. His stride was smooth, and he hit each and every mark. He was a professional who knew that the show had to go on, broken stirrup or not.

Another great coworker was my on-set horse from *Wild Faith,* another Western. His name was Buttercup. Well, let me tell you, that horse performed much like his name. Smooth like butter and cup like . . . like—let's just say I could hold a cup after my ride without my hands shaking as if I'd barely avoided a potentially crippling event.

Buttercup was like the steady Eddy worker you can always count on to show up and do his job. He wasn't lazy like ole Ned and didn't have the excitable inexperience like DC. Nope. Buttercup was go on *Action* and stop on *Cut.* He was a straight giddyup professional.

After our work together, we both went our own ways. I don't dream of Buttercup any more than he dreams of me. It was just a fine example of a good working relationship. Sometimes we can't ask for anything more than that.

# A Forever Friend

## Catherine Ulrich Brakefield

A new neighborhood, a new school, and making new friends are often difficult endeavors for an eleven-year-old. The highlight of my day was spending time with the family's pet—a black three-gaited Saddlebred mare named Black Magic, whom my siblings and I nicknamed Madge. I longed for a friend, a staunch ally in my fight to endure the ups and downs of adapting to a new environment. Madge surprised me by displaying an ornery personality that made the biggest bully in school look docile!

My daily chores consisted of taking care of our hunting dogs, cats, and Madge. I enjoyed grooming her, and Dad sometimes found time to saddle her up to ride, but never as often as he had before we moved. His thriving business took more and more of his time. I missed what our family used to have together. I asked Dad to show me how to bridle and saddle Madge. He showed me once and said not to ride her unless he or Mom was around.

Dad had moved our family from Hazel Park to Warren, Michigan, in the late 1950s into our brand-new yellow brick ranch house built on an acre of land. Dad slapped up a barn for our horse. Behind our home were fields that connected to an orchard and to the home of our friends, Mrs. K and her daughters. We all lived in Warren off Thirteen-Mile Road.

At the time, Warren sported a country-style landscape. Our road was a dirt road that connected to Thirteen-Mile Road. The area was new, and local schools could not handle the number of new students flooding the area. To accommodate the large influx of children, my siblings and I were bused throughout the neighboring communities. Mom stayed busy taking care of my younger sister. Dad left for work before we got up and didn't return until we kids were tucked in bed.

I figured if I could ride on a bus for an hour and a half, I could certainly bridle and saddle our mare. After all, what could be so hard about that? It couldn't be that difficult to insert a horse's bit. But the first couple of attempts, Madge opened her mouth like something was hurting—wow. Finally it dawned on me. I had gotten the bit in backward. Oh well, who would have suspected there could be a wrong and right side to a bit?

Finally I got the bit in and the bridle harness around her ears, and then I spied Dad's large Western saddle. I picked it up and looked at Madge. She hadn't looked all that tall before. No way could I lift this huge thing onto Madge's back. I had ridden bareback a couple of times in our backyard at our old home, so I decided it was time to try it here.

Of course, during those previous rides, the yard was totally fenced in. Not so here. I knew I had to keep a good hold on her reins or else she could spook and run toward the busy Thirteen-Mile Road. I led Madge out of the stable and looked around for a place to mount her.

I tried our swing set. Nope. A bucket? Way too wobbly. Then I spied the wooden milk crate in which we got our Twin Pines milk delivered. I propped this next to my horse. By this time, Madge had figured out that I didn't know what I was doing. Hmmm . . . smart horse. Madge refused to stand still. All Dad ever did was give her two jerks on the bit, and she would wait for him to put his foot in the stirrup and off they'd go. She wouldn't even give me that courtesy.

Then I spied Tip. He was our springer spaniel mix who often appeared more human in his intelligence than most humans. I brought him over and told him to sit, then pointed to Madge. "Don't let her move!" The two eyed each other. That was all I needed.

I got on my milk crate and sprang onto Madge's back. She didn't know what had happened. She started prancing. I held on with my legs, attempting to get my balance. This felt a lot different without a saddle. All I had planned to do was walk. Madge had different ideas. I remembered how Dad took her for a good ride around the property, to make sure Madge was settled down before he allowed us to ride her. That recollection arrived in my thoughts too late.

Madge pranced in place. I snatched a deep breath, remembering Dad's words "Relax and don't hold her too tight. An animal can feel your nervousness." Then I remembered what Mom said: "When you get in over your head, call on your best friend."

*Jesus, help me, please!* I knew if I fell off or stopped now, I'd never get my nerve up again.

I never dreamed I could feel bullied by a horse. I thought my school chums held that honor. I never knew what to say or do when confronted by a bully like the boy who heckled me on the bus and in the classroom or the girl who wouldn't let me sit at her lunch table. Those haughty grins that made me feel unequal to them in every way . . . and it was happening again with Madge.

"Remember," Mom would say, "God made each one of us different, with different talents. You are created to be a unique individual, just like the snowflakes that fall from heaven."

When my report card had only Cs and even sported an obstinate D after working hours over my homework, Mom's warm arms encircled me. She'd say I needn't worry that my younger sister's was all As. I was more athletic, and my sister was more intellectual. "God doesn't grade us; he loves us the way we are." Mom always gave a reason for trying harder, for never giving up, and for not caring if others didn't recognize our efforts. "Just remember, Cathy, all God expects of us is to do our very best."

Madge snorted and flung her head. She wanted to canter. Her long, flowing mane enveloped the hand that clung to a fistful of her hair. The rhythm of Madge's hooves upon the grassy turf sounded like music to my ears. I sat up straighter, balancing on her ample back, lowering my legs to get the optimum balance. I pointed Madge toward the trail, and we were off down the lane I had often hiked with Tip.

Tip followed, I think to make sure nothing happened to me. I really don't know how I stayed on that first time. My adrenaline was pumping. There were no fences to stop Madge or me from exploring. Just the wide-open spaces met our eyes and that distant Thirteen-Mile Road murmur with all those cars zooming back and forth. I gripped Madge's belly firmly with my legs.

The world before me opened up. I say that because from the back of a horse, you don't feel so small. After all, I met my fear, and I now controlled a thousand-pound animal. Her sleek coat warmed my legs as she stretched into a loping canter. I relaxed and enjoyed the rhythm, and I didn't feel alone. I felt exhilarated. I had accomplished a major feat in mounting this powerhouse of horseflesh. The sky was the limit now. I could accomplish anything.

I could even face Billy Boy Bully and Miss Perfect Dresser. I felt so confident that I went to Mrs. K's house. Madge and I trotted right up to their backyard, and Mrs. K treated me to a piece of freshly made cake! I didn't get off, though. I was afraid I'd embarrass myself attempting to remount. Still, this felt like old times when Dad and I rode together.

I waved good-bye, and soon Madge and I were galloping down a mowed lane. I didn't have any clue as to who the owner was, but it was certainly nice of him to make Madge and me this nice galloping trail. I would, however, meet him on my way back home.

When I got home, there was Mom with Mrs. K and a stranger. Could he be the neighbor who owned the mowed path I had galloped down earlier? Something deep down inside said I could be in some serious trouble. Realizing I might have hurt my relationship with Mom devastated my morale.

Mom took in Madge and me at a glance. Her mouth contorted into something like a corkscrew, between laughter and tears. Would she forbid me to ride? Yell at me in front of this stranger? Tell me how disappointed she was in me? I swallowed down the lump in my throat. My new accomplishment felt like a hundred-pound anvil weighing down my shoulders. Mom had the power to crush my accomplishment with just one comment.

Mrs. K, I learned, had driven the man over. They had been talking to my mom for some time. What a shock to find out the man liked horses. I think Mrs. K had much to do with the positive way things turned out. But Mom understood my need to try out my independence. I never told her about the loneliness I often felt walking down our dirt road to Thirteen-Mile Road to catch the bus with the older junior and senior high school students. But her face and attitude said somehow she had known.

After that, the days, weeks, and months clipped by happily for me because of my new friend and confidante safely tucked away in our barn. Miss Perfect Dresser and the other girls didn't bother me, nor did Billy Boy Bully.

I did meet up with a girl who liked to draw horses, so I invited her to my house. Her eyes grew as large as saucers when she saw Madge.

"Haven't you ever seen a real horse before?" I asked.

"I, no . . . I never thought they were so big. You ride her?"

I nodded, feeling larger than life. "I ride her bareback." Nothing would do but for me to jump on and show her my talents.

She was duly impressed. I offered to give her a hand up, with the help of Tip, of course, because no matter what I did, Madge was determined to give me a run for it. After months of riding she still refused to remain standing. It took Tip and me to convince her she had a job to do. But my new friend was not inclined to try and ride her first horse bareback. Nevertheless, this opened up a friendship for me that led to more friends.

A funny thing happened from my experience with Madge. I understood now that bullies had to be managed, sort of like a thousand-pound horse with an attitude. Feeling lonely is just a state of mind. After all, I didn't feel lonely with my horse. So it wasn't people who made a person content. And it wasn't dependence on a horse that could fulfill all my needs and expectations. Madge was just a horse, after all, and she had her own ornery disposition.

Mom was right. My forever friend would always be there when I needed him. That's why she said she didn't worry about me. "Cathy, the leaves can wither and fall, friends can come and go. Only God can fill those vacant spots in your heart."

She also knew God would use a thousand-pound animal named Madge to help me. And he did.

# Gray-Haired

## Sarah Barnum

Y ou're going to put *me* on a horse?"

Grammy sounded both excited and doubtful. I laughed. "If you're up for it, yes. I'm going to take the family on a trail ride."

As the head wrangler at a camp, I enjoyed having the opportunity to expose my family to horses. And Grammy was still active and adventurous at seventy-one years old. When she came ready to ride in jeans, a horse shirt, and a worn blue jacket, I knew exactly which horse I would have her ride. Lucky was a seasoned gray gelding who would take good care of my senior citizen.

But the real reason was because of his color. Grammy had a thing for pale gray horses.

I whistled, cracked the whip, and sent the herd thundering toward the catch pen. The drizzly November day had turned the dust to mud. It sucked at my boots as I haltered Lucky and brought him over to the tie post.

"This is your horse today. His name is Lucky."

Grammy picked her way around a puddle and ran a brush across Lucky's crusty coat. "Oh, he looks just like Cotton!"

I smiled. "Exactly."

I was about eight years old the first time she told me about Cotton. I had just finished cutting all the horse photos out of her *National Geographic* magazines for my horse scrapbook.

"I loved horses when I was your age too," she reminisced. "For a few summers when I was a teenager, my mother and I spent a week at Lake Tahoe. All year I saved my money—babysitting or picking prunes in my grandfather's orchard—so that I could ride Cotton while we were there."

I tucked my horse clippings into a folder as I listened and thought of my own horse savings fund. My allowance and the quarters I earned doing extra chores around the house were starting to accumulate.

Grammy's eyes brightened, and it made her look younger. "Cotton was a beautiful light gray horse, and I loved him. Each summer, I rented him for a trail ride. The trail took about an hour, but once we were away from the barn, we'd go fast and then walk back so the horses weren't too sweaty."

I tried to picture my grandma as a girl like me, flying through the forest on her white horse. I couldn't, really. She was Grammy— gray-haired and grown-up.

That summer, and every summer for the next four years, Grammy's birthday present to me was a week at horse camp. That's when I understood the anticipation she spoke about. I lived for that one week each summer. The rest of the year I played with my model horses and galloped around the playground on my imaginary horse, dreaming of the day I would get to ride for real.

At camp, I went on my first trail ride. My horse? A gray gelding, of course. Maybe Comanche was related to Cotton. He plodded through the Blackberry Pass and Wild Oak trails, nose glued to the tail of the horse in front of him. I didn't care; I was on a horse.

The best part was when he fell behind and trotted to catch up. The trail led us back to the barn far too soon. Even though it was hot and dusty, I didn't want it to end.

I was scuffing my nine-year-old feet down the road to our next activity when I first laid eyes on Lucky. He was hanging out with a handsome bay in the pen on the other side of the road. I pulled out the disposable camera Momma had sent with me and snapped a picture of the beautiful dappled-gray horse.

My one week of horse camp in the summers turned into weekly riding lessons, a college degree in equine science, and a full-time job at the camp where it all started. The horses who taught me to ride—Miramar, Leaf, Amir, Manzanita—were all gray like Cotton. They turned a horse-crazy girl into a lifelong horsewoman.

Grammy supported and encouraged me every step of the way. On Christmas mornings I could count on some horse-themed gift. As a teenager, we took a special trip together to Arizona just to watch the Tucson rodeo, Grammy in her cowboy hat and I adorned with acne and fringe. Not only did Grammy help pay for college, she trekked three hours to visit me at the barn where I competed with the equestrian team.

Now it was my turn to share with Grammy the experience she had made possible for me. She hadn't ridden a horse since Cotton, and I was excited to re-create the memory that had lasted her nearly sixty years.

Lucky turned his head to look at Grammy with the same golden eyes that had looked at me across the fence twenty years ago. His dark dapples had faded to white long ago, and he had matured into the calm and gentle patriarch of the herd.

Grammy eased herself into the saddle and picked up the reins with arthritic hands. I was grateful that the rain stopped in time for our ride. I put Grammy right behind me, and the rest of the family fell into line as we headed out. Lucky picked his way carefully up the same trail where I had taken my first trail ride.

From my place in the lead, I turned to look behind me. Two gray heads bobbed in unison, merging past and present memories into one sweet moment.

"How are you doing, Grammy?"

"Wonderful! This is so special." Grammy raised her fist in a triumph of accomplishment, freedom in her face.

Together, we were both fourteen again, riding our favorite gray horse.

# Wild Thing

## Sarah Parshall Perry

O ne year in November my husband had an idea that was very
much unlike him. He thought we needed a pony.

This was unlike him because for the better part of seventeen
years, he has been working to get farther from horses, not closer to
them. On one of our earlier dates, I dragged him to a horse show
in which I was riding. He smiled gamely at the time, helped me
polish my boots, sat ringside cheering me on. I interpreted these
gestures as approval, and he will tell you it's been a downhill slide
ever since. Now, scattered riding gear, dirty saddle pads, and the
hay in our bed set his eyes to rolling so hard I'm surprised they
haven't gotten stuck that way. Worse? I've gotten our daughter
involved. Because apparently, I hate having money.

That same autumn, our oldest child, Noah, qualified for hippotherapy services under our insurance plan because of his autism.
Hippotherapy is a therapeutic intervention that uses horses to help
children with physical and developmental disabilities work on
muscle development and executive functioning. Horses—wise and

sensitive as they are—are particularly suited to helping children with these challenges.

The farm closest to us with this specialty was over an hour away. So Matt's idea was that we could bring a safe, quiet pony to us. We were renting a farm at the time and had the perfect setup. With more than thirty acres, a few retired steeplechase horses for company, and an eight-stall barn, we had everything we needed. I am a lifelong horsewoman, so having a horse of our own right outside the door made me want to throw a parade. Every remaining particle of the six-year-old me that had prayed for a pony was suddenly revived and obviously on a growth hormone of some sort.

"Leave it to me!" I squealed. "I'll find the right one!"

And I found lots of them. I scanned online classifieds daily. I inquired with friends, posted on Facebook, made calls, and sent emails. From Pennsylvania, to Virginia, to Maryland, we hunted for a very specific animal: one that was solidly built, with great ground manners and a kind eye. We didn't want a fancy show jumper. Looks didn't matter. We just wanted gentle, safe, and good on a lead line. There were pretty ponies and ugly ones; large and medium-sized; talented and green, been-there and pretty-broke-down. I saw them all.

Then, months into our search, I came across the ad for Modoc. He was a red-and-white paint pony, nearly as wide as he was tall. "Quiet," the ad read. "Used in a lesson program for beginners. Never bats an eye." Modoc checked all the boxes on paper.

That Saturday, Matt and I drove to a farm in Pennsylvania Amish Country. I introduced myself to the owner and explained what we were looking for. She led us to a barn where a stocky pony with large eyes and a long face waited quietly in the center stall. His mane alternated red and white like a barber's pole, and the long blaze running the length of his face was interrupted by a horizontal dent that no one could ever explain. I ran my hands over him, feeling for hidden lumps or bumps. I asked the owner to ride him so I could see him go. Finally, I got on him myself. As promised, he didn't bat an eye.

For the modest sum of $500, some signed paperwork, and a handshake, Modoc was ours. I arranged to have him trailered to our farm in time for a Christmas surprise. Wouldn't a pony on Christmas be magical? I even found a red-and-white model pony at a tack store near our house and wrapped it to give to Noah on Christmas morning—as a hint of what was to come.

Once the wrapping paper was done flying, I shoved the kids into boots and jackets and traipsed up the driveway to the barn, sending my mom ahead so she could bring Modoc out into the center aisle.

And then, the reveal. Breath held, I opened the door to the barn. Silence.

"A pony. Wow," Noah said. No gasp. No exclamation. None of the excited hand-flapping that accompanied the early years of his autism. Nothing but a shoulder shrug.

Four-year-old Jesse was likewise not having it. A few pats on Modoc's neck, and he was asking to go back inside for more presents.

But Grace? Well, Grace was in love. She cooed and fussed over him and tangled her fingers in his knotted mane. She asked if his blanket was warm enough, and what we would feed him, and whether the other horses would like him. She asked if she could ride him, right then, and whether—if it got too cold—he might be able to come in the house.

I supposed one out of three wasn't bad.

As we fell into a feeding and turnout routine over our first winter together, Modoc's personality began to bloom. Each day, we'd feed the horses, let them out in the pasture, and clean the stalls. After the first few weeks, Modoc began reappearing in the barn after we'd let all the horses out. He knew that while we mucked, the stall doors would be open and the remnants of any grain and hay would be available for scavenging in the empty stalls. He was just small enough to lower his rotund frame to the ground and slide under the crossbar in a disobedient limbo.

I learned never to muck stalls with my headphones in. Otherwise, I'd find a multicolored rump sticking out of the feed room. When the bitter wind of winter forced us to close the barn doors while we cleaned, Modoc would focus his energies on running off his oversized barn mates when he wanted to eat the rest of the hay we'd thrown down in the paddock. He was outnumbered four to one and outweighed by approximately two tons. But he didn't care.

When the spring thaw came, I rode him for the first time since he'd come home to us. He was a perfect gentleman on the ground, not even turning his head while I gave him a brushing, a pass with the shedding comb, and a thorough hoof cleaning. At the walk and trot, he was likewise a star. Built like a tank with a barrel big enough for a grown-up's legs, he was steady and quiet. It was like riding a couch. All signs pointed to "great choice!"

Until I asked him to canter.

Now, did I need him to canter for Noah? No. Was he ready to canter after a whole winter off? Nope. Did I want him to canter because I thought it'd be fun to see what happened when I hit the gas and what "extra buttons" this model came with? Oh yes. I discovered that Modoc didn't just have a fifth gear, but something more like a tenth. There was no "canter," per se. It was more like a "launch out of the Churchill Downs starting gate and hit the rail at 45 mph" gallop.

An added bonus? Modoc could jump the moon.

While all horses have the natural ability to jump, it takes particular training to encourage them to jump high and well. My guess is that someone had put some time into getting Modoc to learn to fly. In the subsequent weeks, I popped him over a couple of logs in the field. He responded without hesitation, his knees high and square in the air. We went through a stream, past the grazing retirees, and I trotted him up to a wooden coop—a solid, angular fence about three feet high. Modoc fought the bit, raising his head and wanting to run, but I kept him at a trot. At the base of the jump, Modoc finally launched himself in the air, sailing over it with ease and taking off at a gallop on the other side.

It was at this point that I realized I may have gotten more than I bargained for. Our little backyard hippotherapy pony had a bit of a wild side. And I had, unfortunately, flipped the switch to the "on" position.

Once Modoc remembered he had springs, we couldn't keep him contained. Not only did he start jumping the coop in the back of the paddock (twenty-five acres away from our front door, impossible for us to see), he somehow convinced the four retired racers and an off-the-track thoroughbred mare that we'd brought home as a sale project that they, too, needed to shed the confines of their paddock and head for the wilds beyond. After galloping through nearby forests and fields, the band of them would eventually tire, and we would get a frantic call from a neighbor asking if these were our horses standing in her backyard. On many an occasion, we would wake to find six shadowy figures on the front lawn, happily munching grass. Modoc would raise his head to meet our eye, as if to say, "What? It's not like I *made* them do it."

Being so quiet on the ground gave us all the continued impression that Modoc was really a relaxed little dude, and we just needed more time to figure out his quirks. But as I look back on it, he wasn't relaxing. He was plotting. I wrote the pony's behavior off as simply being "fresh" after so much time in the field. I'd plan to ride him down before letting the kids get on him.

Unfortunately, one of those rides I thought I could manage bareback in the middle of summer. While wearing shorts. With nothing more on Modoc than a halter and a lead rope. For a moment, I was that horse-crazy little kid again. The sun was setting on a beautiful July day. The cicadas were clicking, the flies were circling, the horses were snorting.

And I was screaming. Because once I coaxed him from his pasture mates and got the halter on, I had just enough time to swing a leg over Modoc's back and sit down before he took off like he was running the Grand National. It took every ounce of strength I had to hang on for five to six strides before I skidded off sideways like a human torpedo and hit the ground. Hard. Landing on my backside would have been a blessing if I'd been wearing jeans. Any horse person will tell you that you aim to fall where God pads the landing. But as I was wearing shorts, I had 80 percent of my legs uncovered and was perfectly primed for an unfortunate run-in with the dirt and brush. I couldn't sit for a month, and I still don't know what was worse: the pain or the abject humiliation.

After many weeks of work (I worked, Modoc fought) I put Noah on Modoc's back in a closed paddock on a lead line. I stood at his head, ready to grab Modoc's head if he showed signs of taking off. But he didn't. Noah held himself steady with legs that didn't always cooperate. He held the strap in front of the saddle and vibrated with excitement. Modoc the wild thing, true to his original advertisement, didn't bat an eye.

Every day, Noah came to groom Modoc for me in the cross ties before I got on to ride. He refused to let anyone help. He learned that repetitive strokes with the curry comb would increase circulation for Modoc and spread the natural oil of his hair. He learned how to get the pony to lift its foot for being picked. He stood carefully to the side so that he could pull Modoc's tail around and gently tug the comb through it. And when he was finished, Noah would whisper in Modoc's ear and then lean down toward his muzzle, stock-still. When I asked him why, his answer was simple. "I can communicate with him."

After a few weeks, Noah grew tired of riding Modoc. For reasons unknown, we couldn't get him back in the saddle. But his love for Modoc and his belief that they talked to one another remained. Noah was our resident groom. The feeding, the brushing, the letting out and bringing in—it was all Noah. Modoc had in fact become a hippotherapy pony. He just wasn't providing the kind of therapy we'd anticipated. It wasn't the riding that most helped Noah but the responsibility that came with enjoying Modoc's presence at our farm. Noah learned that there was a creature wholly dependent upon him for its very existence. For a child who couldn't follow more than one instruction at a time, for whom the stimulations of his environment were almost too much to take, Noah had come to understand that sometimes caring for a living creature was the antidote to his anxiety and a loud, unforgiving world.

Grace, horse-crazy like her mother, had patiently waited for her turn to ride Modoc. This patience was no small feat for my daughter. To this day, she can wear down an adult like she's getting paid for it. I've seen grown-ups walk into a store with Grace on a promise "just to look" and leave with bags on each arm. Grace is smaller and younger than her brother, but she's always been bolder. She's afraid of two things: (1) spiders and (2) boredom, and she conquers both with flair.

The first few weeks, I walked next to Modoc's head while Grace held the strap on the front of the saddle. True to form, she was quickly bored. After a month, I put Modoc on the lunge line—a long nylon rope that connects to a horse's halter or bridle and allows the animal to be controlled from the ground while the rider learns to be independent with their hands, legs, and seat. This too was a success. Until September, when the sun was setting on a gorgeous Indian summer day.

As I extended the lunge line little by little, Grace sat tall and straight in the saddle. I can't say whether Modoc spooked or was stung by something as we walked around the first bend in the ring. But he bolted. And he didn't stop. With every ounce of strength, I pulled in the line as hard as I could. My hands burned under my gloves as the line snaked outward, and I fought nine hundred pounds of panicked animal for the safety of my daughter. My heel spun in the dirt as he continued to circle me while Grace screamed. God protected her—and when she finally came off (later, she would tell us she simply let go), she landed perfectly in a soft bed of pine needles. Nothing broken, nothing sprained. Grace had had the wind knocked out of her but lived to tell (brag) the tale.

To this day, I can hear her desperate voice in my ear. I suppressed my terror in the moment, but later creeping in was the feeling of having failed her somehow. I have ridden long enough to know that animals are unpredictable, that only so much can be controlled. I knew then that it was time to let Modoc go.

As our experiment with hippotherapy and pony ownership came to an end, I wondered about Noah. He had been the driving force behind our peppermint-colored pony, and I worried that as attached as he was to his animals, the breakup would be a painful one. I needn't have worried. My mother bought Noah not one but two guinea pigs for Christmas a few months later, and as the reign of Bubblegum and Frodo began in earnest, all but a few memories of Modoc were cast aside. That is, until the spring, when Frodo disappeared from his cage and we spent the better part of a week looking for him. Then, Noah very loudly proclaimed that we should have kept the pony.

"Because at least they're easier to find!"

When it came time to sell Modoc, his ad read

Pony "Modoc" for sale: 12.2 hh quarter paint pony who jumps 3′ with snappy knees. Great ground manners, pace for hunting and jumpers, has jumped coops, logs, crossed water. Easy, easy keeper. Perfect child's hunt or jumper pony. Price reduced for quick sale.

If you're a novice to the horse world and have never read a sale ad, you wouldn't necessarily know that this ad can be summarized as follows: "Cute pony. Kind of fast. Not for beginners."

Grace went on to ride at a formal lesson barn six months later. Despite her harrowing experience, she overcame her fear to start with a professional on a much smaller pony with twenty years of experience teaching small riders to be brave. Now Grace jumps full courses of fences on both ponies and horses. Every hotheaded pony with a naughty streak is right up Grace's alley. Reminding us often of how she held on to Modoc until she got tired ("I could have held on longer if I were bigger!"), she's now riding everything she can get her boots on. Grace is not only strong but brave. Our wild thing helped make her so.

Modoc was sold within a few months. He spent some time being shown in Western Pleasure and later was used in another lesson program. He was ultimately retired to a farm in northeast Maryland where my friend boarded her own horse. Seeing a picture of him on my friend's Facebook page one day, I asked her about the pony. I told her he looked familiar. Did she know anything about him?

"Oh!" she said. "His name's Modoc. The kids love him. He's super patient with all the petting and brushing. But he's a bit of a handful. He's a real pig with food and tends to jump out of his paddock. We finally figured out he had to be pastured with the Belgian draft horse, because he's the only one that Modoc doesn't intimidate."

And here, I burst into laughter. Because after many years, it appeared Modoc was still a very wild thing.

# Callie Had a Secret

## *Yvonne Haislip*

I dreamed of having a horse all through my childhood. But I was raised in a home with five kids, and having horses was out of the question. We had dogs and cats, but no horses. I did ride a horse once when I was fourteen and was bucked off, but my dream of owning a horse never faded.

Finally when I was in my forties, that opportunity fell in my lap. My friend Mandy had two horses. One was a mare named Pepper, white with pepper spots all over her. Pepper's daughter Callie was a beautiful Connemara paint and Appaloosa—black with white spotted sides, white face mask, and white spots on her stomach. My friend had bred for Callie, but she wasn't attached to her, and she decided to sell her.

Mandy knew I'd wanted a horse all my life, and she invited me over to ride. This was only my second time ever to ride a horse. Callie was four years old and saddle-broke, but she was spirited and lacked some basic manners. She didn't listen well. She did what she wanted and could be a little up in your face about it. But I liked her and agreed to buy her.

I will admit I felt some fear for my safety. Besides having no horse experience, I'd had a bad car accident a few years before and since then had been very protective of my physical situation. So I didn't rush into taking Callie home. But I took the risk to learn to ride Callie. I learned how to pay attention to her body language and how to handle her.

My husband had agreed to our having a horse, but he was working overseas at the time, so I prepared for Callie's arrival myself. During the three weeks my husband was away, I dug postholes and put up fencing and made a corral. We had an old shed that was full of my husband's junk, so I cleaned it out and put in electrical wiring. I took down a wall for horse entry and made a two-section barn, one section for my husband's work area.

And then I brought my horse home. This was all new to me, so I waited a few days before riding her. I liked to go in the barn at night and listen to her eat and pet her head. Eventually we went riding, first in the yard, then in the back acres, and soon into the woods.

A couple years after Callie's arrival, I needed to be away for a few days. During that time, and against many odds, Callie somehow got together with the stallion next door. She came away from that experience pregnant. I didn't realize it at first—not until she was four months along and her belly started growing. I was thrilled, and I immediately expanded her building and consulted the vet.

The vet gave me her due date, which would be around my twenty-eighth wedding anniversary. My husband and I made no big plans for that upcoming date because I refused to miss this birth.

Three weeks before Callie's due date, I hung a hammock in the stall and started spending nights there. Callie would steal my pillow or my blanket while I was sleeping and dump it on the floor. She did this over and over—she loved attention. But when she slept, her head was right over my hammock. Every day and night I touched her belly and talked to her and to her baby.

On our wedding anniversary, I got up early and made enchiladas because family was coming over. It was a green and lush August day, and we all sat outside so I could keep an eye on Callie. As night came on and people left, it turned chilly. I was putting away leftovers at around eleven while my adult daughter Michelle checked on the barn. All of a sudden, I heard Michelle scream—I dropped the leftovers and got to the barn just as baby Secret was coming out.

Callie was a first-time mother, and she seemed shocked. Her newborn was a palomino paint, very tan, with a white curly mane and tail. She had white spots on all four legs and the same markings as Momma.

Since this would be my first foal, I had done some research about imprinting. So right after the birth, I began interacting with her. I told the baby her name was Secret. I put my hand in her mouth, played with her tongue, and played with her belly and her legs. I brushed her mane and tail and acquainted myself with her hooves. I put my own zippered sweatshirt on her and kept it there for a couple of days.

Within the first hour, Secret was on her feet. Callie began to nurse the now-standing filly. While that went on, I took down the hammock so the baby couldn't get tangled in it, and I made a new bed for myself on the floor. Then I sat on my pallet and watched mother and daughter bond—nursing, smelling each other, staying close.

I remained seated while I watched, leaned back against the wall, cross-legged. When Secret was done nursing, I talked to her and called her by her name. She watched me and listened to me. After a bit, little Secret took steps toward me—maybe about twenty of them to come alongside me—and then did the most wonderful thing. She dropped herself right on top of me and curled up like a baby.

Secret's full body was on me, from my knees to my chest, her long legs folded up. It was like holding my own newborn—though this was a large and lanky one. There's nothing better to me than holding a baby on my lap—even a little filly. I had a children's blanket nearby, and I covered her with it. I could sense Secret's sweet disposition already. My daughter happened to walk in and see this. She backed out very quietly and returned with the camera, and then she left us alone.

At first I was a little nervous about Momma Callie in all this. As a rule, she was a handful. Would she agree to my intimate interactions with her baby? But Callie simply walked over and stood beside me. She seemed to know that Secret was in good hands in my lap. Maybe she welcomed the help.

By now, it was two in the morning, and all of us were tired.

Secret stayed curled in my lap, and she went to sleep.

Callie stood over us both, and she went to sleep.

And then, so did I.

# Conquering Fear

## Loretta Eidson

Growing up, I spent most of my summer breaks visiting my grandparents on their farm in west Tennessee. The way they lived fascinated me. Watching Grandma scrub clothes on a rub board and then toss them in a large cast-iron pot sitting on a fire out in the yard exposed me to the simplicity and yet the complexity of living on a farm.

As an eight-year-old, I was amazed that my grandma's eggs came from the henhouse and her butter came from a churn. Back home in Memphis, eggs came from the grocery store, butter and milk too. But here, apples on the farm came from the apple tree, and purple grapes came from the vine growing along the fence that divided the garden from the front yard.

Grandma made biscuits using flour from a cloth sack and a scoop of lard instead of popping a can open. She cut them with a metal biscuit cutter that had a red handle and placed them on a round cast-iron skillet. Then, she pinched sugar with her fingers and sprinkled the top of each one and baked them in her wood-burning oven. She called them angel biscuits.

Grandpa said the blessing and thanked God for the food each time we sat down to eat. My parents did that too, so it was nothing new. I couldn't help but sneak a peek at Grandma, though. Tears dripped from her cheeks during the prayer, and she'd repeat, "Yes, thank you, Jesus."

Every morning and every evening, Grandpa left the house to tend to the animals. It didn't matter if he'd been out on his tractor all day, he still went to see about them. The closest thing to an animal I'd ever owned in the city was a goldfish, so the enormous size of his livestock intimidated me. He had more animals than I'd ever seen outside of the zoo.

Cows, pigs, chickens, dogs, and a single horse.

My cousin Mitch always joined me for a couple of weeks out of each summer. He and I were the same age, but I figured he knew more about animals than I. When he arrived, he ran straight to the old pine tree in the front yard and started climbing. I scampered up behind him and sat on a small branch in the very top. The view encompassed the entire acreage of my grandparents' property, including all the farm animals.

I spotted a pond in the distance, and even at my young age, hanging out in that tree day after day, I noticed a pattern in the livestock's grazing habits. The horse didn't always keep the same schedule as the cows, but they mostly hung close to the water in the mornings, wandered to the far end of the pasture by midday, and back around to the pond in the late afternoon. I assumed that's where the cows and the horse got their water because I never saw a water hose stretched across the yard. In fact, my grandparents' home didn't even have an outside water faucet. They drew water from a well.

When Grandpa returned home on his old red tractor from plowing the fields, I begged to go with him to milk the cows, hoping to get a closer look at the horse. Every time I asked him, he'd tell me he wasn't going to baby me, that he had work to do. It didn't matter; I clung to his shirttail as he walked through the herd of cows to the barn carrying four empty galvanized milk cans. I'm sure if I'd been younger, I would have crawled up to his shoulders in fear of those oversized animals, especially the big bull, and the horse that looked as big as a dinosaur.

"Does that horse have a name, Grandpa?"

"All my animals have names." He chuckled. "That's Nellie. She's an old, overworked mare."

"Do you ever ride her?"

"No, but your daddy and uncle used to ride her when they were younger. She pulled the plow in the truck patch for years."

"What's a truck patch?"

"It's that big garden behind the smokehouse where your grandma gets her vegetables."

Grandpa opened a creaky wood door at the barn and let me hang out in the corn crib so I could watch him while he milked the cows. Occasionally, warm milk hit my face, and I'd scream. Grandpa's shoulders shook with laughter. I moved and stood with my hands on the splintered planks and watched Nellie moseying around just outside the barn, swishing her tail. Those brown spots sprinkled on her white coat were beautiful. Could I ride her? I shuddered at the thought, but I couldn't wait to get back to the house to tell Mitch that our daddies used to ride Nellie.

Later that night, as I snuggled in the feather bed and listened to the hum of the oversized window fan, Mitch tiptoed into my room. We came up with a plan on how the two of us could mount the tall horse. Goose bumps crawled across my arms as fear swept over me. Grandpa said she was old, so I reasoned that she couldn't go very fast and there'd be nothing to be afraid of, right? Anticipation got the best of me, and I couldn't sleep.

The next morning, I followed Mitch to the pine tree and watched for the cows to make their way to the far end of the pasture while Nellie stood around the pond. Grandpa left on his tractor, and Grandma stayed inside to can peas. Perfect timing.

We shimmied down the tree and ran down the path toward the barn. I gripped the barbed wire fence, daring myself to crawl under the bottom strand of wire. My heart beat against my chest, and I hesitated. Mitch called me a sissy. That did it; I had to prove I wasn't afraid.

I looked up into the clear blue sky and shielded my eyes from the sun. *God, I'm afraid. Please don't let the cows get me!*

I took a deep breath and rolled in the dirt under the wire and caught up with Mitch, holding on to the back of his shirt until we reached Grandpa's new barn. It stood further out in the pasture than the old one where Grandpa did his milking.

Flies buzzed around cow patties, and wasps zipped by my head. I covered my nose with my hand, hoping to avoid the pungent smell that was a dead giveaway the cows spent a lot of time in that area. The chickens didn't seem to care that their lives could be in danger. They just pecked the ground and clucked.

> *The wind of heaven is that which blows between a horse's ears.*
>
> ARABIAN PROVERB

Again, fear swept over me when I realized that's where Grandpa fed the horse and the cows. My eyes shot to the sky as I folded my hands, ready to pray, and I did pray, silently, but I didn't want Mitch to hear me verbally confess my fear.

He found a rope just inside one of the barn stalls, jerked it down, and walked slow steps toward the horse. I tiptoed behind him, ready to bolt should anything go wrong. He threw the rope around Nellie's neck and led her to the barn. I was proud of my cousin's bravery.

## Side Saddle Up!

Many view the side saddle as a more modern invention, but it dates back thousands of years—as far back as the sixth century, in fact, where the Greek god Hephaestus is depicted on a vase riding side saddle. For centuries, the side saddle was viewed as a more modest choice for women when compared to riding astride. And, *ahem*, in years past it was even suggested that female thighs were "too rounded" for the astride position. Some cultures went so far as to suggest that it was physically unhealthy for a woman to ride astride.

When we picture a woman riding side saddle, we often think of a Victorian woman in a smart riding habit complete with tailored jacket and riding crop. And while it's true that the side saddle was enormously popular in the Victorian era, it certainly wasn't without its downfalls. Quite literally. Because if a woman fell while riding side saddle in a traditional full skirt, she could be dragged to her death. Sadly, there were numerous accounts of that happening. Hence, stylish riding habits with wrap-around skirts (or open-backed skirts called aprons) swiftly grew in popularity. Heavily boned corsets worn beneath the riding jackets gave Victorian ladies the correct (and beautiful) silhouette. But it also gave them a propensity for fainting due to the restriction of the garment. Ah well, no one said riding was for wimps!

The "planchette" side saddle positioned a Victorian woman facing completely to the side with her feet resting on a step, allowing her to display her lovely gown. But in this not-so-secure position atop a horse, women could only sit and watch (#nofun). They had no control over their mount and were led on the horse by stable workers.

Gradually, improvements in side saddles allowed the rider to leisurely walk the horse, while still other side saddles equipped with pommels allowed women to take to the hunting field and to jump. Around 1950, the side saddle fell sharply in popularity when it became acceptable for women to ride astride—and to wear trousers. We've come a long way, baby![3]

Tamera Alexander

Standing beside Nellie made me feel small like one of those chickens. My head measured up to her mid-belly. I moved away from a possible kick and followed until Mitch tied her to the planked barn door. A bridle hung on a rusted nail close to a bale of hay.

I climbed up on the planked gate and scooted my feet across the board until I was even with Nellie's neck. Mitch slipped the bit into her mouth and passed the reins up to me. I nervously held them with one hand and hung on to the gate with the other while he climbed up beside me. He slid one leg over the horse's bare back and scooted forward to make room for me. Nellie's head bounced, she took a step forward, and her tail swished. I wanted to back out, but then Mitch would fuss at me the rest of the day and call me names.

He took the reins from me and gripped the gate with the other hand to keep her steady while I slid on behind him. To my surprise, her body was so broad, or rather, my legs were so short that my heels didn't have anything to grip. Before I could jump off, Nellie pulled away, and off we went, walking through the pasture. Hooray, we did it.

I wrapped both arms around Mitch's waist, but my body still bounced like popcorn. At least Mitch had the reins and both hands full of Nellie's mane. Mixed emotions swirled inside me. When I realized we were getting closer to the cows, it meant we were too far away from the barn. I insisted we turn around and go back.

He reluctantly agreed and pulled the reins to the left. No sooner had Nellie turned around, she went into a gallop toward the barn. I had been wrong. Being old hadn't slowed her down at all. My body tossed like a kite in the wind while I hung on to the only lifeline I had, Mitch.

"Quit holding so tight," Mitch yelled. "I can't breathe."

"I . . . I can't. I'm falling." Screams escaped with each bounce.

"Stop. You're pulling me off."

Nellie knew just how to remedy the situation. She headed for the only tree between us and the barn. Before I knew what had happened, leaves were in my mouth and I plummeted to the ground, still hanging on to Mitch. Ouch!

He jumped up and yelled at me for pulling him off, but I was so afraid the cows would come after me that I took off running toward the barbed wire fence. I crawled to safety while my body trembled. My skinned elbow didn't compare to what could have happened.

Mitch stomped toward me, grumbling and fussing. He wasn't hurt either, just mad. Laughter filled the air, and I turned to see my sister standing close to the chicken house, holding her stomach, laughing. When did she arrive? That meant Mom and Dad were there too. Would I be in trouble?

"Do it again," she said. "You looked like a rag doll flying through the air. Come on, do it again. Mom and Dad watched the whole thing. They laughed when you jumped up and ran."

"I've had enough horseback riding for the day." I glanced back to see Nellie standing by the barn gate with the reins hanging to the ground.

While stopping at the fence with a mean look, Mitch picked up a stray pine cone and threw it at me. He turned around and went back to Nellie and removed the reins before running toward the house. I chased behind him and followed him to the foot of the pine tree. He picked up another pine cone and tossed it across the yard.

"Want to see what Nellie's doing now?" I asked.

"Okay, but I'm still mad at you."

I jumped and grabbed the lowest branch, wrapped my legs around it, and climbed to the top of the tree. Mitch followed. The wind tossed us around on the small limbs. Nellie stood between the barn and the pond, grazing on grass, swishing her tail as though nothing had happened. She looked majestic, like a dream, and I'd found a new love for her.

My eyes met with Mitch's.

Laughter erupted.

"Want to do it again tomorrow?" A big grin spread across his face.

"Sure." I covered my mouth with my hand and giggled. "I'm not afraid anymore. I prayed, and God took my fear away."

# Fooling the Magician

## *Tracy Joy Jones*

I've often thought that making a new friend is like standing at a rope bridge to unexplored territory. What stories am I about to discover? What adventures lie on the other side of the bridge? I might find danger that will make me wish I'd never crossed over in the first place, but more often than not, my life is changed by seeing the world from another point of view.

As I stood on the front porch, waiting for my new friend, Kendall, to pick me up, I couldn't help wondering what kind of adventure awaited me this time. From where I stood, her side of the bridge looked a lot like an old Western movie. She wore a cowgirl hat everywhere she went, denim jeans, and genuine leather boots layered with the dirt and wear of real work. Her east Texas accent was warm in its drawl, and her skin was tanned and freckled from the sun.

Kendall smiled easily, and when she invited me to go horseback riding one Sunday afternoon, I immediately agreed. I had that relief you feel when you're sitting alone in a room full of people and someone finally joins your table. It doesn't matter who they are; you're just so glad for the company.

As a newcomer, getting an invitation to do anything with a local felt like an offer of mercy. And although I didn't grow up with horses, I've always loved them. An afternoon spent meandering over pastures and trailing through the piney woods of East Texas sounded idyllic. As a bonus, I just might make a friend.

By the time Kendall arrived at the house, I was so excited I practically flew out the door and down the wooden steps, not even giving her the chance to exit her truck.

"Hey, Kendall! Thanks for picking me up." I climbed into the passenger side of her old sky-blue Chevy truck and began quickly searching for a seat belt.

"Oh, don't bother. Grandpa ripped them out."

"He ripped out the seat belts? Why?"

Kendall shrugged matter-of-factly at my question as if to say, *Why does it matter? They're already gone.*

Admittedly, I was a city girl. Seat belts were a life and death necessity, not just a suggestion. However, I was in the country, and this was not the moment to freak out in front of my new friend.

I forced myself to relax as her V-8 engine roared to life, country music blaring from the speakers. A minute later, we were roaring down a two-lane road, Kendall tapping her well-worn boot against the rusty floorboard, while I tucked my white canvas shoes under the bench seat. As cute as they were, my Converse shoes seemed a sure giveaway of my lack of horseback riding experience. Then again, the horses wouldn't care, and maybe Kendall wouldn't even notice.

Ten minutes later, the truck slowed as she pulled into an empty gravel parking lot. A small stable sat at the far end of the clearing, but the majority of the space was taken up by a large metal enclosure. Two yellow barrels sat at each end of the ring, and tethered to the fence stood the largest horse I'd ever seen in my life.

I expected Kendall to pull around to the stables, but she parked her truck by the stallion.

"Come on!" My new friend jumped from the truck, her face glowing with enthusiasm. I exited more hesitantly and slowly followed her to the metal pen. Why were we here? Where were the trail horses?

"So, what do you think?" Kendall waved to the stallion, pride evident in her eyes and her tone.

"He's beautiful," I answered honestly. The horse was one of the loveliest I'd ever seen and by far the largest. Sleek, glossy flanks, a glorious mane of chestnut hair, and massive white socks for coloring, he had all the markings of a thoroughbred. But it was his jaw-dropping size that had me biting my lip with nerves, my breathing increasingly shallow.

*Please, God, don't let this be Kendall's version of horseback riding.*

The chestnut stallion stamped impatiently in the ring, pulling defiantly at his tethered reins. I took a step backward. This couldn't be right.

My eyes searched the stables beyond the barrel racing ring, hoping to see a couple of sedate mares saddled and waiting to take us on a peaceful trail ride. But a second later, my fears were confirmed as Kendall climbed the rails of the fence and dropped into the ring with the beast.

Now, if I was being honest, I'd never ridden anything but trail horses or well-tamed mares, and they'd all been shorter than I am. I couldn't imagine riding a horse like the one in front of me. First of all, it was way beyond my skill level, and second, I'm afraid of heights.

I followed her up the rails with sweaty palms and a racing heart, but I couldn't bring myself to follow her the rest of the way. Instead, I perched on the top rail and watched her walk to the horse's side. It was only when she untied his reins that my fear turned to panic.

"I've had him for a little over three years now. Everyone said he was too tall to barrel race, but he's surprising them all. He's just over seventeen hands."

Wait a second—barrel racing? Surely not. I could only nod and smile as she continued explaining. I knew horses were measured in hands. I knew the horse in front of me was enormous, but other than that, I definitely didn't speak the language of thousand-plus-pound, thoroughbred, barrel-racing monsters.

Kendall, on the other hand, was cowgirl cool beside him. Her hands reached above her head to lovingly caress the corded muscles of his massive neck. I couldn't help being impressed by her courage, even wishing I was like her. Or at the very least, that I wasn't so terrified.

I forced a strangled smile as he shifted his weight impatiently, wanting to be in motion. I shifted my weight further back from the fence rail, ready to make a break for it if he did. But Kendall didn't seem to notice either his restlessness or my nervousness and went on to tell me how she had rescued Blue Magician from the racetracks. I'd never seen a prouder parent, standing with her oversized baby. She stroked the thick mane with tenderness, and he seemed to stand even taller in response.

From the relative safety of the fence, I smiled at the appropriate moments in her story and kept my face pleasantly interested. In other words, I pretended beautifully. I even asked questions, all while trying to reason with my fear. She just wanted to show me her baby. I had nothing to fear. And then she said the dreaded words.

"So, are you ready to ride him?"

Panic froze the smile on my face. I swallowed hard, trying to breathe normally. I'd never been less ready for anything.

Now, what I should have said was "No, thank you."

What I actually said was "Sure."

The instant the word left my mouth, I wanted it back. What?! Why had I agreed? Some hideous desire to impress my new friend had hijacked my brain. I wanted her to like me, but I had no business getting on that horse. My head felt slightly woozy as I considered Magician's size once again.

And then stubborn pride kicked in on top of my fear. I could do this. I would just pretend my fear wasn't real. After all, I always claimed to be up for any adventure. When would I ever get this opportunity again? This was the perfect chance to conquer my fear of heights and large animals, to make a memory and a new friend—or more realistically, to shorten my life span by seventy years.

I took a deep breath and almost threw up, but my pep talk was sort of working. In an insane moment of bravery/stupidity, I hopped down from the fence, my canvas shoes sinking into the red east Texas dirt. Kendall took a step toward me, Magician in tow, and suddenly I knew the terrible danger of positive thinking and pretending. The horse was as big as one of those hairy mammoth replicas at the museum; his gleaming brown coat rose like a wall in front of me. It was all I could see. His back stood above my head; the stirrups sat above my waist.

Now, I've never been a very flexible person, even on a good day, and that really should have been another clue to Kendall that I did *not* need to get on this horse. I gamely proceeded to lift my foot as high as it would go and hop on the other foot for balance while reaching my toes for the stirrup. If I were in Kendall's boots, I would have been laughing my head off, but I'm not sure Kendall had a sense of humor.

She just frowned, calmly considered the situation, and said, "I'll get a block."

*Oh, great.* A block of what? I had no idea. All I knew was Kendall had left me defenseless beside a thousand pounds of muscled horseflesh, and I clearly had no business being there. I scampered away from him as quickly as I could.

A minute later Kendall was back with a hollow wooden block that she placed under Magician's stirrups. That's when I knew I was in real trouble because this was actually about to happen. I didn't speak, my pride and desire to please strangling the words. Instead, I climbed onto the block, as if to a hangman's noose. My feet somehow found the stirrup, and I landed astride a genuine thoroughbred racehorse. For the briefest moment, I felt a thrill of exhilaration. I'd done it. I'd conquered my fear.

And then Magician shifted beneath me. My mouth went dry as I peered down at Kendall from what felt like a million miles away. I was holding on to a thin band of leather that was supposed to control this massive animal, and I absolutely knew that I was *not* the one in charge. The horse had all the power, all the confidence, and something about the look in his black eye as he shook his head at me said he knew it. I wanted to make myself (and the horse) feel better about the situation, but all the platitudes you usually say to a pony felt wildly out of place on the back of a racehorse.

*Who's a good boy? What a pretty boy!*

In my limited experience, trail horses need a lot of encouragement. This horse did not. He was already the king of his world. What he needed from me was respect and confidence. What he got from me was bravado and fear.

Kendall removed the block and then backed away, waiting. Apparently, I was supposed to ride now with no further instruction. It was in that moment that I made one of the biggest mistakes I could have on a racehorse: I dug in my heels.

Now, as every amateur trail horse rider knows, if you don't give a trail horse a little kick with your feet, they don't go. Years later I would learn that you never, under any circumstances, kick a racehorse, and that day I learned why.

A thousand pounds of muscle bunched beneath me and instantly sprang to life at a full sprint. One instant I was still, the next he was screaming down the enclosure. I thought he'd turn at the barrel. Wasn't that what he was trained to do? But he just sprinted past it and headed straight at the fence.

The world slowed, and certainty hit me. This monstrous horse was about to jump the fence with me on its back. I had no doubt the horse would make it. I would not. I'd never jumped anything in my life, and all my instincts warned that this was not going to be a successful first try. And what would happen on the other side of the fence? Would he tear into the woods dragging my lifeless body? Death was imminent, and my survival instinct finally motivated me to act.

"Whoa!" I shouted like an idiot, pulling back on the reins in terror. He didn't stop. What he did do was slow, just the tiniest amount. At the last possible second before crashing into the metal rails, he turned to the side, and only then did he come to a sudden stop. My leg was so close to the rails, it was almost pinned against it. Kendall ran toward me.

"What are you doing?" she yelled at me instead of her horse, grabbing the reins from me and stroking his traitorous neck. "Can't you ride? You can't be afraid on a horse like this. Horses sense fear."

My stomach roiled as I hurried to dismount, my eyes wet with the sting of her rebuke. So much for my pretenses. The drop to the ground was a terrifying distance, and my legs almost collapsed underneath me as my feet hit the dirt. I staggered as I tried to move to safety.

"I'm so sorry," I muttered to Kendall, still trying to breathe, adrenaline still pushing my heart as if it were on its last leg in a race for survival.

Kendall's features were hard and tight as she led Magician a short distance away, and I felt our fragile new friendship splinter like a broken bridge. I wasn't who she thought I might be, and she'd almost killed me. It was a rough beginning.

She mounted easily, without the block, and proceeded to show me exactly what that horse was capable of doing. The pounding of his hooves rolled like thunder against the red earth, yet Kendall stayed perfectly in control of Magician's every movement. For the next half hour, I watched them race in figure eight circles around the yellow barrels, while I cowered on the fence top, humiliated and angry.

But in my heart, I knew it wasn't really Magician or Kendall's fault. I should have been honest with both of them. Sometimes courage is simply admitting that you don't have it all together, you don't know what you're doing, and that you're afraid. In my eagerness to make a friend, I had sabotaged the journey by not being real.

I wonder how differently my friendship with Kendall might have gone if I'd simply said, "I've never ridden a horse this big. I'm pretty nervous. What do I need to do?" We might have formed a genuine bridge of friendship. Instead, pretending to be something I'm not *almost* had me jumping fences, my lifeless body trailing an impossibly fast racehorse through the woods.

I've never ridden another thoroughbred since that day, but Kendall and her Magician taught me that friendship takes honesty for the real magic to happen. And the next time a friend asked me to go riding, I made sure to bring my authentic self along for the ride.

# Spirit of My Seventies

## Chris Kent

During a fall elk hunting trip in northern New Mexico I came to realize just how much I had missed equine companionship. Riding horseback for hours with our guide through the Jemez Mountains rekindled that old love, the one that had been ignited by my first horse, a gift I received more than a half century earlier on my eighth birthday.

Time on horseback had always provided me a sense of freedom and independence, a view of the world that could not be found any other place. Now that we were living off the grid in a log cabin tucked away in the spruce and hardwood forest of the remote Upper Peninsula of Michigan, not to mention me being well north of sixty years old, owning a horse again was not only highly improbable but also not so practical. We had no cleared land, no barn, and no known source for hay.

On the last day of the hunt, a spectacular crisp, clear October day, I handed the reins off to our guide with a farewell handshake and a reluctant stroke to the neck of my borrowed horse. The guide looked at my husband, nodded knowingly in my direction, and said, "She'll have a horse by spring."

It wasn't spring, but it was a sweltering afternoon the following July when a silver grullo gelding, Blues Tiger Doc, arrived at Bruleridge, our Upper Peninsula home. He had muscular hindquarters wrapped in tiger stripes, dapples dotting powerful hips, and silver highlights dusting his black mane. What were his thoughts as he peered between the thin slats of a red stock trailer at the welcoming committee of my husband, Kaiser our German shorthair, and me? The narrow view of his new home was of towering aspen and spruce forming a wall around the small barn and newly cleared paddock.

Startled by the piercing bray of a donkey, we realized the horse was not alone. He had arrived accompanied by an entourage of traveling companions—two tawny-colored, wiry-haired donkeys, their oversized ears flapping from side to side without control, and a curly-coated blond mini wearing his surly disposition in his flattened ears. My surprised reaction was quickly dismissed by the former owners. "I didn't want him to be lonesome on the ride."

His reluctance to travel should have been clearly evident by the accompanying reinforcements if I had not been blind to any roadblocks. When the gate of the stock trailer swung open, a hind foot cautiously touched the fresh ground, then a second, the crown of his head pushing against the fiberglass roof as the horse's body thrust backward, then rose slightly on planted hind feet. His ebony eyes flashed as silver-tipped ears moved in constant motion and flaring nostrils exposed an intense shade of pink. The big animal strained to take in all aspects of his surroundings. Nervous energy was trapped in every inch of his sixteen hands as he danced at the end of the lead rope. At that moment my level of confidence regarding our ride together, this horse and me, into my seventies, was faltering.

In the weeks that followed, the boundaries of our relationship were tested. The nickname Tigger, given to him by previous owners, didn't fit this splendid animal. Thus he became Spirit. Supernatural, apparition, mirage, specter, phantom, ghost, a manifestation—I was to learn he is that definition, he is them all. I was reminded often by a friend I might have chosen a name like Smokey or Spot, something more definitive of the appropriate persona for a "senior" rider's horse.

Right away, Spirit would brace his feet, refusing to enter his stall, the stark white showing at the edge of his black eyes evidencing his fear or uneasiness. He had difficulty understanding my simple explanation that wolves living in the surrounding forest might find him delectable as he stood alone in the paddock at night.

The first appointment with the vet was a disaster. A no-nonsense woman, gravelly voice, armed with a twitch and little sympathy for 1,200 pounds of frightened horse, she never got close enough for even a cursory exam.

The initial visit by the farrier was disaster number two. Spirit spent most of the time on two legs, the farrier ending the session telling me Spirit was not the horse for me. I should be concerned for my safety.

Then, soon after, came a ride on the trails through the woods that included a sudden bolt by Spirit throwing me back across those dappled hips, giving me a view not recommended when riding horseback, a view of the toes of my worn leather boots set against blue sky and aspen tree tops. My white knuckles gripped the reins as I strained to pull myself back upright in the saddle. My husband's voice, just audible behind me, said, "Are you all right?"

I mentally took stock of my condition. Everything seemed to be working, nothing hurt that much. Good sign. A second nervous, just perceptible sound from behind me, "What just happened?"

"I'm okay. Just give me a minute." I made a second inventory of my body. Spirit danced sideways on the narrow trail, head high, ears nervously moving as I stroked his neck, trying to calm him and myself.

Coaching, cajoling, reassuring became the pattern of our days. Spirit and I spent countless hours since that day in the woods in a constant series of "dance lessons." Those pirouettes have taught me an increased awareness and appreciation for the intelligence, curiosity, and affection of this animal. I have learned patience and perseverance as we have danced together. He too has learned—to trust me and to better understand what I am asking. We have waltzed, done the two-step, sometimes a fox-trot, or even a mamba, but finally my partner has agreed to let me lead.

I found a round pen to be a very effective environment for Spirit. It allowed us to establish leadership, respect, and communication. I was able to control his direction and movement in a relaxed environment. He soon began turning his inside ear toward me, licking his lips, and watching me for cues. Providing him the freedom to make choices allowed him to comfortably invite me into his world, to his dance.

A new farrier reminded me, "Pay attention to his actions; often there is a physical cause." He demonstrated this as he diagnosed a minimal level of arthritis Spirit had in his knees that caused him pain if his hoof was pulled toward the outside when trimming or shoeing. He now stands perfectly for a new set of shoes.

Hours on the trails with the constant flutter of grouse and the startling rustle of deer bounding through the brush have calmed his initial fears in the woods. There are still days we dance, we test each other with a new step. However, every morning he greets me with a long whinny when I open the back door, and each evening he calls to me from the gate to remind me he wants a few minutes of my attention.

Daily I am fascinated and entertained by the antics of my silver grullo gelding. His curiosity is insatiable. He looks out barn windows, watches any nearby activity, snoops through items left in the barn aisle, and searches jacket pockets for possible treats or treasures. His life is best without change. Routine and sameness comfort Spirit; he notices even the most minor of alterations.

He joins our shorthair in the love of retrieving and sometimes carries a ball, his feed tub, or even a small water container around the yard. He steals hats or gloves from unsuspecting people. He grabs a glove in his teeth, moving just out of reach, shaking his head and again moving off just enough to keep the game going. If Spirit is around the tractor, my husband has to be sure the brake is set and in neutral as Spirit discovered the accelerator and enjoys revving the engine. The joy he brings with his ongoing antics is an unexpected reward, a paying forward for those challenges or new dance steps we face.

I know we will have our future setbacks. He will never be the "bomb-proof" horse that was advertised. And he's not the horse by definition an old lady should be riding. However, he has taught me that horse doesn't truly exist. A moment of complacency at any age on any horse is the prescription for disaster.

Conversely, he too has taught me the value of a new challenge in this period of my life. He has taught me patience, perseverance, and a thirst for new equine understanding, and he has rekindled that old love of the redolence of a horse on my hands and clothes. I have accepted with regret the need to use a mounting step to climb on his back. I know my aging mind must be alert every moment I spend with him. I understand the need to exercise additional caution to protect my brittle bones. In spite of all this, I plan to exhaust the coming years learning more every day regarding the purpose, disposition, personality, and ability of my horse.

On my seventieth birthday my husband asked, "What do you want to do to celebrate?" It was an easy response that came without thought. No thanks to dinner at a fancy restaurant, a diamond ring, or something new for the house. "I want to spend this spectacular autumn day on my horse in the woods with you and your horse."

And so we did. A canopy of blazing gold and crimson leaves clung to the trees overhead while a matching carpet blanketed the earth under the horses' feet. Leaves created a cacophony of sound as hooves moved rhythmically along the trail. The sky was brilliant dazzling sapphire with just an occasional wisp of silken clouds propelled by a gentle breeze.

After several hours of riding we stopped along the river for a respite. Spirit hung his head over my shoulder as I rested on a downed log, his chin in my lap, his black ebony eye next to my face, a glimpse into a soul. There was a harmony that day between body and Spirit, an *esprit de corps* we had not experienced before. And so began my ride into the next decade on the back of this remarkable being—my Spirit.

# Let Go of the Reins

## *Shannon Moore Redmon*

Fred was the first pony I ever rode. His coat was the color of chestnuts, and a white diamond graced the front of his nose. He was smaller than most, and maybe that's why I loved him so much. A seven-year-old girl with ponytails could control him. Larger horses scared me a little.

Fred belonged to the kid across the street. His daddy owned acres of land and filled it with horses, full-grown ones mostly. However, he bought this pony for his son. I was a bit jealous and wanted one of my own, but Momma wasn't gonna clean up after an animal that big.

However, when Neighbor Boy decided to mosey over on the back of his steed one day, I transformed into the cowgirl of my dreams. Who the animal belonged to didn't matter, as long as I got to ride.

I still remember the creak of the saddle the first time I climbed onto his back. My skinny arms struggled to pull myself onto the seat.

"Just throw your leg over and use your arms to pull yourself up," Neighbor Boy said.

"I'm trying. I'm not strong enough."

My arms burned with effort, and a drop of sweat dripped down my temple. "I can't do it."

"Yes you can. You just ain't tryin'."

"Am too," I shot back.

Caty, my cousin, stepped up to Fred's side. "Here, I'll help ya."

She boosted me up. I flung my leg over and sat up. This wasn't right. I was facing the rear of the horse.

Neighbor Boy burst out laughing.

"Silly girl," he said. "You don't know how to ride a horse. Turn yourself around."

I managed to maneuver myself into the proper position and reached for the reins.

Neighbor Boy kept them from me. "Ain't no way I'm letting you steer. I'll lead ya."

I wanted to be in control of this pony, like most things in my life. "I can do it," I said and reached for the reins again.

"Nope."

I tried to grab them again, but he stepped back. My hand fell to my side. Fred was his horse, and Neighbor Boy insisted on leading me around the yard. I folded my arms across my chest and shot him my hardest stare. He didn't budge.

The pace started out slow, just a couple of circles. My body wobbled forward and back as Fred waltzed, grazing on blades of grass between each step. The sensation was strange. I fought to keep my balance and hoped Neighbor Boy had fastened the saddle on well. He wasn't the brightest sometimes, but at least he seemed to know about horses.

Mother watched from the porch for a few minutes, her eyes wide, encouraging me to hold on tight. Neighbor Boy faked kindness when she was around, keeping Fred's walk to a slow, steady pace.

But then she went inside, and Neighbor Boy began to jog. Fred changed his gait to a trot. I bounced along, clinging to the pommel. It wasn't much to hold, and the cracked leather scratched my fingers.

"Slow down," I said.

Neighbor Boy didn't listen and kept right on moving . . . faster. Fred didn't seem to mind the change in pace, except he could no longer snack on the sweet grass now passing quickly under his feet.

Neighbor Boy increased his speed until Fred was in a full canter. I screamed for him to stop, but that only seemed to amuse the kid. He laughed and ran faster. My heart raced, and breaths came in short spurts. I curled my fingers into Fred's silky mane and prayed I wouldn't die today.

Through the yard, down the hills, and into the pine trees Neighbor Boy went. I ducked with Fred to keep my head from hitting the lower limbs. My cheek pressed into the animal's neck, and his muscles moved with strength. Somehow, we both managed to keep our skulls from being cracked open with passing tree branches.

Fred followed his leader with grace and strength. Even though he'd never raced through my yard before, this pony kept his rider safe. He never toppled or reared up. He dodged the obstacles in our path. The ground was steady under his hooves, even down steep grades. The tighter I clung to him, the more we moved as a unit. My bobbles smoothed into a coordinated ride.

Finally, the jaunt came to an end.

I slid from the saddle, and my feet hit solid ground. I gave Fred a pat or two, silently thanking him for keeping me safe.

Then I spun on my heel and faced Neighbor Boy. Heat rose to my cheeks, and several choice words ran through my mind. My lips parted.

"When can I go again?" I asked, a wide grin spreading across my face. Even though I was terrified, I trusted Fred. He never let me down. He kept me safe. We became one, moving in sync.

Fred chomped down on my mother's flowering bush, not giving the exhilarating outing a second thought.

Mother rushed from the house. "I think it's time you took that animal home now."

Neighbor Boy nodded and swung up into the saddle. Across the road he went, taking Fred back to his big green pasture. Mother began to stomp the uneven divots in her yard.

"I thought that boy went way too fast with you on that horse. Weren't you scared?"

"No, Momma, it was so much fun."

Fred only visited us a couple of more times. Momma didn't like cleaning up the steaming lumps left in her yard. I'd watch him through the picture window wandering with other horses in the green pastures across the road. But time passed and we all grew up. Neighbor Boy moved on to bigger horses and I moved on to bigger dreams.

I'll never forget the feeling of freedom my first pony ride provided. Sure, it was a little bit scary, somewhat dangerous, but Fred never let me down. He offered protection, strength, and comfort once I chose to trust him with the ride. God provides me with the same and so much more. Sometimes it's good to let go of the reins and move as one with him.

# Michigana Perry Goes to Wyoming

### DJ Perry

Every summer the local cowboys of Elk Rock, Wyoming, looked forward to the arrival of the pretty girl from Michigan. Her mitten-state lingo, groomed blonde hair, and Detroit fashion were a deep contrast with the local style of practical, dusty, and rustic.

The pair of ranch brothers we'll call "Hoss" and "Little Joe" to protect their outlaw identities could barely muster a possum's pinch of hospitality when meeting the pretty girl's plus-one: me. Unfortunately, I was not one of her plucky girlfriends from college who loved horses, Hank Williams, and *Hee Haw*, looking for summer fun. Nope. She instead brought her boyfriend.

From gritted teeth and crushing handshakes, I entertained question after question from the brothers. It felt more like *Dusty's Trails* detectives giving me the third degree—wanting the who, what, where, when, and . . . *Wait! They're probing for a weakness.*

"You like horses?"

The fact is, I had quite a bit of experience with horses. For three summers I had attended Cranhill Ranch horse camp. The rage at that age for most was windsurfing in the cold, cold, cold—did I say cold?—lake. But the horse camp usually had forty-plus cowgirls who made the experience enjoyable for us five smart teen boys. Note: This attraction to these girls got me in this Elk Rock situation to begin with.

"Horses? Yes, I love them."

This reaction was met with a silent nod. "You ever ride a bull?" The casual dialogue seemed to be turning sinister, but I have a brain always looking for the improbable but possible story.

The following day the ladies had a planned day of shopping. This meant many hours driving to some small general store. One of the brothers whose chores were done offered to save me from the shopping trip by showing me the local sights. I was unaware that "show me the sights" meant following big Hoss dangerously up a forty-foot crevice. Back and feet pressed against rock, shimmying up a cliff face to a small ledge. The other side was a certain death drop, one of those sights that put weakness in your legs.

On the climb Hoss imparted to me a tale about skeletons found in the crevice. I worried they might one day find the body of a visiting Michigan guy as I descended underneath my meat-and-potatoes guide, who caused a small rock-a-lanche. I managed to avoid any skull wreckers that might have granted me a tragic ending.

After another nightly Wyoming cowboy ritual of listening to Garth Brooks under the most comprehensive starry sky I've ever seen, I was taken to a nearby riding ring. Finally horses? Not unless this horse had grown horns. This was *not* the ride I was looking for. This was a far cry from my past summer camp experiences.

Brashness has led many young men to get cocky. But when you get a side eye from a young bull . . . things change. It's funny how a couple thousand pounds of muscle can be humbling. I disappointed the two provoking cowboys by bypassing their insults and refusing to participate in what I saw as a plan to harm and mangle me.

I decided to lay low a few days and not take up the daily invitations by the brothers: "Do you want to go shoot guns?" and "Do you want to go check out the family hunting cabin at the top of Elk Mountain . . . where a bear has been breaking into the smokehouse?"

Guns. Bears. Sorry, busy. But yes to horseback riding. I was curious if we had to capture them like wild mustangs. No, they gave me their mother's horse. Well trained. Let's call her Belle.

Belle was a powerful beauty of brown with black around her nose and legs. "Walk her around and retighten the saddle," I insisted. Horses hold their breath when being saddled. If you don't get them to exhale and retighten the saddle, it will often slip, sending riders crashing to the ground.

My knowledge of this horse trait brought a "foiled again" look from one of the brothers. His disappointment was barely hidden under his wide-brimmed hat. After a spit of chaw, he moved to tighten the saddle. Once the saddle was tightened, a slap on the horse's rump let us know we were ready to ride.

I got in the saddle, ready for a good trail ride taking in the local sights akin to ole Yellowstone Park with its majestic mountains and rugged terrain. But that slap on the rump was like the crack of a starting gun announcing the Gold Rush. Belle bolted like the Headless Horseman himself was chasing us. I tried to summon my inner cowboy and control this horse as I had controlled many others on several occasions. Belle bit down hard on the bit and ran like lightning across the rugged terrain.

The barn and the rest of our party became mere dots in the distance as Belle ran directly toward a steep hill. The horse did not slow but increased her speed. I felt her body tighten as she launched herself airborne. My hands forgot all my cowboy training and grasped for the brass-covered horn like a kid on a grocery store penny horse. I adjusted one hand to grab a handful of black mane just to keep my balance.

Belle's back hooves clawed to keep us both from falling backward. Once she found her footing, she started zigzagging up the hill like a mountain goat.

I had never felt more out of control. Even steering a car on black ice felt more secure. Terror turned to laughing, a funny reaction in retrospect. I thought I would have been screaming, but even with no one around to see, I was still trying to stay calm.

Belle arrived on top of a mountain, and the view was breathtaking—God's glory. Belle started running across the top of the flat mountaintop, and I could see the approaching drop-off. It was a really, really, really steep drop to jagged rocks several hundred feet below. I found myself praying *Please, God, let this not be a suicidal horse.*

My prayers were answered when at six feet from the edge, the horse sharply barrel-turned. I almost flew from my saddle, but my kung fu grip on her mane held tight. Belle continued this running back and forth and barrel-turning just moments from a drop that would be a sure death. Around the sixth turn, Belle stopped and pawed the ground as Brother Hoss atop an all-black horse came riding up. He explained that Belle had never been ridden by anyone except his mother, who just happened to be a professional barrel horse rider.

Never ridden? Barrel! He asked if I wanted to change horses. *Yes!*

Hoss dismounted and held my reins as I got off Wild Belle and on Black Jack. Before Hoss could remount Belle, the two horses started fighting. I'd been less than sixty seconds in the saddle of this new horse, and he was doing a Lone Ranger rear up and swinging hoofs at my former horse.

Once the horse conflict settled, we slowly started to make our way back down the mountain. As we passed an old wagon left for dead in the desert, I watch a large bee fly toward us and attack ole

Black Jack. The first couple tail slashes altered the course of the would-be stinger but not the determination of the little bee. That sting resulted in wild twisting, kicking, and bucking as seen in a professional bull riders rodeo.

Using whatever athletic ability I had mixed with a healthy fear of being dropped on my head, I slid off the horse, landing on my feet. Black Jack threw a few final kicks in the air before running toward the distant barns. The brother offered Belle back, and I refused, happy to walk.

Maybe it was my John Wayne cool dismount. Maybe I stayed on the bucking bronco for a full eight count. Maybe I had survived some kind of trial of the cowboys. Whatever it was, I gained some respect. From that point on, they seemed to accept me.

But that horse Belle? Not so much. She had never been ridden by anyone but one rider up until that day. That was the day Michigana Perry came to Elk Rock, Wyoming. Giddyup.

# Showing It Alone

## Susan Friedland-Smith

My heart horse, DC, was a gorgeous dark bay thoroughbred with a blaze. He could be kind of a stinker in daily life, but he lived for horse shows. His show name, Adonis, suited him well, and he knew how to turn on the charm at just the right time when the judge was looking.

After a move from the Chicago area to California, a grad school program, and a career change, I decided to take my beautiful former show horse to a little local show, just for fun. We had not competed in several years, but it seemed like a good idea.

Someone at my boarding barn had a trailer and was going to take her horse, so she offered me a ride. I had never done a horse show alone before. By that I mean without my mom, sister, and especially a trainer. But I was a seasoned horsewoman, although my show career had been on hiatus. I certainly knew how to walk, trot, and canter a horse. I viewed this as a chance to challenge myself and have a "learning experience."

The day before the show I bathed DC and said a prayer that he wouldn't lie down in a pile of his own brownish green apples and that he wouldn't sleep so soundly that tiny cream-colored shavings would cling to his fuzz of a forelock and mane and tail. I rubbed his forehead and scratched his chin a bit and gave him a kiss good night and took home his saddle pad to wash.

The next morning I arrived at the barn early. The row of horses I had to pass to get to DC's stall had their heads down, intent on eating their breakfast. When I called his name, DC courteously took a few steps toward me, ears perked, still chewing. Then he returned to the more interesting pile of green stems on the ground. I let him continue to eat as I squatted down to wrap his legs with puffy white pads that looked like diapers and followed that up with black standing wraps. I had already put only my essential brushes, a hoof pick, and fly spray in my yellow plastic brush box. I put the saddle, girth, bridle, and brush box in my car and was good to go—except I had forgotten my saddle pad, which I realized once I got DC settled at the showgrounds.

One of DC's shortcomings was that he could not be tied. If he was tied, he would pull back and break his halter. Better to have a broken halter than a broken horse, however. He sported a nylon halter with a leather crown piece so that the halter would snap in an emergency.

Because this was essentially a step above a schooling show, I didn't have to braid him. I had rented a stall since I could not tie him to the trailer. I was the only one who had rented a stall since everyone else had someone to take turns holding the horse.

I walked past several horses tied to trailers, happily munching from a hay net. I didn't say it to them but thought, *Don't you know all it would take is one quick tug and you could be free?* I threw some hay into the box stall, which was a few hundred feet away from the arena. DC whinnied and whinnied and whinnied a series of shrill calls. He was so loud. It was embarrassing.

I found someone to loan me a saddle pad, and then I decided I should turn DC loose in the round pen about three hundred feet from the show ring. Maybe he could get rid of some of his nervous energy by frolicking for a few minutes. He did just that, huffing and puffing and shaking his head. To my horror, the horse show announcer announced, "The round pen is not open during the show. You need to remove your horse from the round pen."

Now I was not only the lady with the horse who wouldn't shut up, but I was the rule breaker. Which was odd since I'm very much a rule follower in real life. It's just unwritten rules I'm no good at. Had there been a sign that said "No turnout," everything would have been good.

Somewhere in the midst of this chaos, Gabriel showed up—not the angel, but a friend from church. Gabriel was a single dad I had gotten to know through our young adults ministry. He had always wanted to learn how to ride horses, so he had asked me to join him a few weeks earlier when he embarked on a mission to purchase boots and a riding helmet for taking riding lessons. I needed to head over to the show secretary's table to register for my classes and get my number, so I left DC in his charge. Although Gabriel was green around horses, I figured he was a guy and therefore strong. I assumed even with limited riding experience, he probably knew how to hold a horse. It couldn't be that tricky to hold a lead rope, but I hadn't accounted for just how tricky it can be to hold the lead of an unsettled horse at a showground.

As I filled in the papers, DC started his fretful whinnying again. One of the ladies at the registration table made a snide remark about "that bay horse." As I filled in the registration form I said, "I'm trying to enter 'that bay horse' of mine into the hunter class," hoping to make her feel embarrassed. But it was my turn again as someone shouted, "Loose horse!"

I turned and surmised DC had spooked and pulled away from Gabriel, as he was trotting proudly much like the Black Stallion in

## Cincinnati

Ulysses S. Grant rode a series of horses during the War Between the States, but his preferred mount was Cincinnati. This magnificent chestnut stallion came from a long line of racing thoroughbreds. His grandsire was a famous horse named Boston. He was sired by Lexington, the fastest four-miler in the nation. Cincinnati stood seventeen hands high and in Grant's estimation was the finest horse he had ever seen.

Grant was so fond of Cincinnati that only two other riders were permitted in the saddle, Admiral Daniel Ammen and the president of the United States, Abraham Lincoln. Grant wrote, "Lincoln spent the latter days of his life with me. . . . He was a fine horseman and rode my horse Cincinnati every day."

After Appomattox, Cincinnati remained with Grant. He lived long enough to be stabled at the White House when Grant became president of the United States. Cincinnati has been immortalized in paintings and sculptures carrying his famous rider. Captain Samuel H. Beckwith said, "No artist could paint the beauty of his horse in the midst of action, when the curb was required to hold him back."

Eventually retired, Cincinnati lived out his days on the farm of Admiral Ammen in Maryland. Cincinnati died in 1878.[4]

Claudia Wolfe St. Clair

the scene where the boy was trying to tame him. DC was beautiful when he was loose. Thankfully, DC's wild freedom was short-lived as a nearby good Samaritan successfully grabbed the dangling lead rope.

I thanked the helpful stranger and told Gabriel not to worry about it. I was the one who at this point was a bundle of nerves: my horse had been broadcasting his unease by whinnying across the whole showgrounds, I had been publicly busted over the

## Traveler

Robert E. Lee rode Traveler, a dappled gray American Saddlebred, throughout the War Between the States. Traveler was as famous as his rider. He was steady in the heat of battle, often pressing forward as troops advanced.

After the war, Traveler remained with Lee in Lexington, Virginia, when Lee became president of Washington University. Before Lee's family joined him in Lexington, he wrote, "Traveler is my only companion, I may say my only pleasure."

In later years Lee looked back on the war experience. He wrote, "I do not see how I could have stood what I had to go through without solitary rides on Traveler. No matter what my cares or troubles were, I put all such things out of my mind and thought only of my ride, of the scenery around me, or of other pleasant things, and so returned to work refreshed . . . and in a better and stronger condition."

In the final months of Lee's life, his health declined rapidly. His doctor appealed to him, "You must make haste and get well. Traveler has been standing in the stable so long he needs exercise." But Lee's riding days were over. He died peacefully that night. A treasured horse without his rider feels the loss. Traveler followed Lee a few months after. Both are interred in Lexington, Virginia.[5]

Claudia Wolfe St. Clair

loudspeaker for using the round pen, and now my horse had been *the* "loose horse"! What was going to happen when I mounted and rode him in the show ring? Maybe it was stupid to think I could go to a horse show by myself. Where was Joanne, my trainer from Illinois, when I needed her? And my mom?

To make matters worse, I had noticed earlier that there was a spectator camped out at the far end of the show ring with a large blue beach umbrella. In most every arena I had ridden in, DC would select one specific spot of the arena that was his personal nemesis. If he was feeling very spunky, he would let out a full-blown spook, snorting and shying away from the terrifying corner. If he was feeling a little more subdued, he might simply drift in toward the middle of the arena or stay near the rail but turn his face slightly opposite of the proper bend, suspiciously eyeing the scary region of the rail.

I would prepare for such shenanigans by maintaining a solid yet gentle contact on the outside rein and keeping my inside leg very close to the girth with pressure on his side in an attempt to keep him straight. I would try to focus my attention to a point beyond the scary spot. And breathe. The irony in riding is there is so much going on behind the scenes, thoughts, subtle muscle movements, ring strategy in an attempt to make for a beautiful ride that portrays the horse as though he is moving effortlessly and everything is his own idea.

When I mounted DC, it was as though I came to rest on a wad of nerves, not my lovely equine companion of ten years. My heart was fluttering even though my brain was telling me to be calm and communicate confidence to my horse. He needed me to be the adult in this situation.

DC held his head high, like a sentinel scanning a king's domain. I walked him in the most forward walk he was capable of to the schooling area and began warming up for impending disaster. Earlier in our show career, I lunged DC for about forty minutes at the trot to get him to relax, and by the end of the session he was mellow enough to behave civilly. I did not have that luxury that day. So I attempted to re-create what had been a successful strategy Joanne had taught me a decade earlier. And so began our marathon trotting exercise. The tricky part was that I knew if I trotted him too much, I would be useless, as my fitness level was no match for his.

Right as I was about to depart the schooling area to sheepishly ride "that bay horse" into the show ring for our first class, a familiar, cheery "Hi, Susan!" broke into my internal pep talk.

I could have cried. Dana and Patrick, two dear friends who didn't even know each other, had shown up at the same time to support me. Dana had her camera in hand. Gabriel had had to leave just before I started riding.

"I'm about ready to go in." I pointed out where they could stand along the rail to have a prime view of the forthcoming entertainment. My horse, who had been a bundle of raw energy up until that point, decided to use his power for good once inside the show ring.

The announcer intoned, "You are now being judged at a walk."

I took a deep breath and tried to shove my heels down further and stretch my spine up taller. I put on a smile. Not a senior picture or wedding day smile, but the corners of my mouth turned up a bit, reflecting the sheer delight and pleasure it was to be on such a grand steed.

There were only about five other riders in the arena, and I did my best to space myself out so that DC and I could dazzle the judge. We neared the umbrella lady on our first lap, and DC didn't bat an eyelash. In fact, he perked his ears forward and kept looking straight ahead, very receptive to my subtle squeezes on the reins.

When the judge was not looking, I talked to DC. I don't think he needed any reassurance, but I did. I knew that if I talked, I would have to breathe. And if I had to breathe, my body would hopefully relax.

We began to trot at the announcer's bidding. I could feel the correct diagonal but still glanced down, with my eyes only, keeping my head level and looking ahead. I was fine but didn't want to take anything for granted. DC's springiness popped me out of the saddle ever so slightly, and I went forward with the motion and then gently for a millisecond until I sat down to repeat the cycle of posting UP, down, UP, down.

The judge called for a walk, and I knew what was next. So did DC, but he didn't let on. After a few strides, I regrouped, shoving my heels down against the stirrup irons, shortening my reins an inch, and caught a glimpse of my two dedicated fans standing at the edge of the arena.

"Riders, please canter your horses. Canter."

I barely grazed DC's right side with the heel of my boot, giving a little squeeze to the left rein, a squeeze just like the end of prayer when you're holding someone's hand in church.

My show horse pushed off his hind end and burst forward into a left lead canter. "Good boy!" I whispered. He flickered his ears back for a second, listening to me, and then focused his ears forward again to show off for the judge. I sat tall and proud. None of the earlier problems mattered—the forgotten saddle pad, the announcer publicly scolding me about using the round pen, DC's blaring whinnies across the showgrounds. We were there to perform for the judge and for the crowd. But mostly for each other.

DC's elegant stride swallowed the ground, and I maneuvered around other slower horse and rider combinations. It wasn't a race, but there was something gratifying about forging ahead of the others. My carousel horse kept the same rhythmical hoof beats going until the judge called for a walk. I sat down deeper in the saddle and pressed all of my fingers firmly together on the reins to make them signal the transition. DC slowed down and resumed a forward, showy walk.

The judge called for a reverse, and I had a slight worry that approaching the umbrella from the new side might be cause for reaction. Not so. We repeated the same energetic trot followed by the right lead canter. The entire ride should have been videoed because it was textbook perfect. In spite of that, I had low expectations. After all, I had been the show black sheep.

DC stood like a gentleman as we awaited the results. He turned a bit to the left and a bit to the right to check out his competition close up. He chewed the silver snaffle bit just a little bit and then looked at the judge with his ears pointed forward. I swear he was posing for her.

There were six of us in the class, so I figured DC and I would at least get a ribbon. The announcer revealed the placings beginning with sixth place. Our number was not called. He went through all the other placings then called, "In first place, number 282, Susan Friedland riding Adonis."

I leaned forward to accept our blue ribbon. Then DC and I trotted to the gate, where my friends were waiting.

"Congratulations, Susan!" Dana cheered in her mild Louisiana singsong. Patrick smiled, congratulated me, chuckled, and congratulated my horse. DC was less interested in the words of praise and pats than in sniffing the new people to see if they had any carrots. I gave Dana the ribbon and returned to the arena for the next class: equitation.

My confidence had risen sixteen hands high!

The next class was almost the same as the first, although I was more relaxed. And when it was over we had won another blue. By the end of the day I had won the championship for my division. Even though it was "just" a schooling show, I was as delighted as if I had won at Madison Square Garden. DC was quirky and sometimes unruly, but I had him mostly figured out at that point. We were a true team. My heart was bursting with love and my spirit with joy.

The best part of this horse show was that about two weeks later, a friend from my barn said, "Susan, I got an email from the organizer of the show. They put out a monthly newsletter, and she was wondering if she could get a picture of you and DC to include in the next issue."

I happily emailed the picture to the contact at the show, thinking, *The black sheep became the superstar!*

# The Meaning
# of an Heirloom

## *Tisha Martin*

Sometimes what we treasure comes in the form of our love for a pet. For me, that was the love of horses. And like we do with a precious family heirloom, we pass down to others the things we love.

I was eight years old when I was introduced to the world of horses. Two of my dear friends had horses, and my special-needs twin sister and I would visit their farm often to ride the sleek and tender standardbred horse, Dream. The four of us spent many summer afternoons riding through tall fields of grass or sprinting across bean fields after fall harvest. The whoosh of the wind in your face and the horse's mane floating on that wind is a gift of love no one can ever replace. The horse I rode became my own dream because soon I realized I wanted my own horse.

When I was a little older, I convinced my younger siblings that they wanted a horse too. We dumped all our loose change, allowance, and money from summer fund-raising sales into the horse fund. I'm pretty sure, though, I was the one who contributed the most to the cause because like Billy Colman and his hounds in *Where the Red Fern Grows*, I could only sleep, dream, and talk about getting a horse.

Every weekend, my dad brought home the *Tradin Post*, and I scoured the Pets and Livestock section for a horse—any horse—for sale. I don't know how many calls I made or how many times I was disappointed to hear "I'm sorry, the horse just sold" on the other end. With each disappointment I only grew more passionate and determined about finding just the right horse. I'd read plenty of *Western Horseman*, John Lyons, and *Horse and Rider* magazines to know the personality type I needed and what vices to watch out for. This horse was going to be loved by not just me but my siblings too, and we certainly didn't need a naughty one.

Mom did take me and a few of my siblings to see one pony. He was black and a little bigger than a Shetland, but he had the temperament of a stormy sea. My eleven-year-old brother and I brushed the pony, and the entire time he stood with his ears flattened. Thinking it was just a quirk, I saddled up, and we took him out to the driveway for a ride. Before I could even mount, the pony swished his tail and was prepared to kick with his hind leg.

"Watch out," my mom warned, grabbing my six-year-old brother and moving away from us.

I cued the horse to move away from me, pulling its head around so his nose would touch his shoulder, as I'd read you should do when dealing with a naughty horse. In the end, I didn't even ride that pony because of his sour personality. Whether or not he was simply having a bad day—as do people—I decided this probably wasn't the right pet for me or my siblings.

So it was back to the classified ads. One ad boasted that a tricolored pony had been Amish trained. Could this be the one? I asked my mom to call on this one because I just knew it was the right one, and I didn't want to hear that it was sold. It was easier to get difficult information secondhand.

"Oh, she is still available," Mom said, and I clasped my hands in excitement. "When can we come see her? This Saturday?"

This Saturday! My dream was about to become a reality. Amish-trained horses didn't stick around long, so I knew this had to be the right one. At least I prayed it was the right one.

We drove five hours south with a horse trailer in tow. Yes, it was that serious, almost like a dating relationship about to turn into an engagement or waiting for a grandparent's last will and testament to be read, hoping for a piece of treasure by which to remember the loved one.

> *Horse sense is the thing a horse has which keeps it from betting on people.*
>
> W. C. FIELDS

Molly, a pretty tricolored pony, was tied to a fence rail outside the main barn when we arrived. She perked her ears as I approached her, and I held my hand out flat, letting her sniff. Good sign. "Sorry, no treats, but we did come to ride you," I said.

All my siblings—down to the six-year-old—rode Molly that day, and we even harnessed her up to the cart that she came with and drove around the yard. Molly didn't kick, pin her ears back, or swish her tail in disagreement. These were all very good signs.

"Do you think we should take her home?" Mom asked. "She seems like a good pony."

The excitement overwhelmed me like a rushing waterfall over pretty rocks.

My search had ended. My horse savings fund had reached the price of the pony: $600. And I had a pony to love forever . . . and to share with my siblings, of course.

Over the next six years, we rode Molly everywhere—literally over the river and through the woods—and enjoyed her company.

Five of us children would straddle her and ride down the lush farmer's paths to the clearing in the woods and have an afternoon snack of oatmeal cream pies and peanut butter bars. Molly, her black mane shining in the summer sun, contented herself with grazing as she swished her tail.

My siblings grew older and began to get interested in other things—hunting, fishing, playing the piano—and I was back to riding alone. I was glad I'd saved most of the money because it made the ownership and responsibility that much more special. But I really wished for someone to share my love for horses and to ride with me.

When my baby sister, Savannah, was six months old, I took her for a quick ride down the driveway and back. Molly seemed to understand that a wee one was on her back and was ever so gentle as she plodded across the gravel driveway. As Savannah grew older, we went on longer rides around the farm. Then as a toddler, she'd beg to ride Molly, and most afternoons that's how she took her nap. When her head began to bob against my arms holding her in place, I would take her to the back door and wait for Mom to come out and take her to bed. But it never worked. Savannah would wake up in Mom's arms, reach for Molly, and say, "More horse. Me ride." And another round we'd ride.

A big smile always crossed my face. Savannah loved riding as much as I did. I had my riding buddy, and yet another dream came true. When she was six, Savannah started riding with me every afternoon. On school days, we got up before the sun, made toast and sprinkled it with cinnamon and sugar, and went for a morning ride. On the occasional Friday afternoon, we'd cart Molly and drive the three miles into town to the library to return some books and check out movies for Friday Family Night. But we had to stop that once our rat terriers and Rhodesian ridgeback caught wind of the adventure and joined us. I couldn't be responsible for the dogs too, and we didn't need a fiasco because

I wasn't about to tie them to the cart like they did in the Old West with the livestock.

Over the next few years, I acquired more horse friends. I traded a manure spreader for a paint mustang named Sister, who was a yearling. I hoped to train her. Sister's sky-blue eyes, alert and curious, captured my attention the moment she stepped off the trailer ramp. Pink nostrils pulsed, sensing new smells of animals and territory. I ran my hand down her slender white neck and noticed nicely balanced markings on her chest, back, and hindquarters. Her red-tipped ears twitched like radar sensors as she listened to unfamiliar noises. Despite her alertness, she was quite gentle.

During the summer of 2007, Savannah helped me with the saddle and bridle during the groundwork training stage. She petted Sister while I saddled up. Seeing the treasured wonder in Savannah's eyes brought joy to my heart. True sister bonding in more ways than one.

"Thanks for helping me," I said.

Savannah beamed, stroking Sister's nose. "Sister's almost asleep."

As gentle as she was, Sister wasn't without her shenanigans. One afternoon as I was riding her around the yard for our fourth time in saddle, she dumped me. Like a bronco, she dumped me over her shoulder onto my back. Hard.

It was my fault, though. I'd been guiding her right and left to teach her general riding etiquette. Apparently I was miscommunicating, and she didn't quite understand. There I was, on the ground, staring inches away from her pulsing nostrils sniffing me.

I wasn't about to let her win the dumping battle, just as she wasn't about to let me win the miscommunication battle. After catching my wind, I limped for a bit because my back muscles were tight as a lug nut on a wheel. Sister followed me like a puppy. Of all things. I mounted, and we continued our ride.

I don't have Molly or Sister anymore. I sold them just before I headed back to college, but the tight bond we'd formed with each other taught me a lot about loyalty, trust, and friendship, almost as if they were my sisters.

My real sister, however, carried on the love for horses after I went to college. Savannah treasured and tended the horses at our friends' family farm and is now involved in 4-H with Scout, a pretty piebald who has the tricks of a clown up his sleeve—I mean, hoof. Family heirlooms don't have to be tangible; they can be as intangible as the love for a horse and very much treasured from generation to generation.

# Ransom

## Connie Webster

I was nearly fifty when my friend Sharry came with me on a journey to find a good, quiet horse for my family. I hadn't been riding very long and was still a nervous novice. Sharry had had horses almost all of her life, so she was wise to what I should be looking for—a quiet, late-teens horse, laid back with lots of training. What horse people call a "steady Eddy."

At that time I had my mare Shiloh. My daughters and I rode her, but she was much too petite for my 6′3″ husband, Mike, to ride. Sharry's friend Dawn wanted to sell a mare that she said would be great for us, so Sharry and I went to check her out.

When we got there we realized this mare would not be a good fit, but Dawn happened to have another horse on her farm. This one wasn't hers but belonged to an Amish gentleman who lived up the road. The young gelding was born on the Amish farm and trained as a cart horse. There were plans to sell him to the "English," as he was too flashy for the Amish. They prefer to have solid-colored, less noticeable horses, and this horse was a paint.

The gelding was not quite two years old, and while Sharry and I knew that would be too young for me, we were curious. We followed Dawn to another pasture and into a large decrepit old barn with the strong smell of old manure and musty hay. The barn was bursting with a cacophony of animal sounds. There were dogs barking, sheep bleating, horses neighing, and geese honking. It really was a cluttered, noisy, unsettling place, but there in the midst of that dark, dusty barn was a round pen. In it stood a tall, handsome tricolored paint with a white face and beautiful blue eyes. There were four stallions stalled to the side of the gelding's round pen, calling and rearing and bucking in their stalls. But the young gelding simply stood there quietly, taking everything in and watching us.

There was a hole in the roof of the barn, and as I was looking at Ransom, a ray of light came through that hole to shine down on him standing so quietly. Horses and people are often drawn to one another, and I feel beyond a doubt that at that moment Ransom chose me and I chose him.

So I brought Ransom home to my farm. Shortly afterward my husband's employer of almost thirty years closed their doors. Here I was with two horses—one of them needing daily training to become a trustworthy trail mount—and now I needed to work more hours at my job than I ever had before.

Anyone who has been around young horses knows they can be explosively reactive, especially when brought to an area they are not familiar with or where they don't feel safe. Ransom was not that way. Still, it was not a good idea for my husband, who knew almost nothing about horses, to interact with a two-year-old gelding right away. But Ransom seemed to draw my husband to himself. This was something new for Mike.

Before I knew it, Mike was taking Ransom on walks with a halter and lead. First they walked around the backyard. Then they ventured down the road and over the hill and through the woods far from our farm, sometimes for hours at a time. Ransom proved to be uncommonly calm, and he and Mike journeyed along and became friends. I'm sure that this friendship was not only good for helping Ransom to feel safe and calm in diverse situations but it was excellent therapy for my husband.

As Ransom settled in, we found that he also had quite a sense of humor. While I was clearing up the paddock one day, I noticed our barn cat getting a drink from the water trough. Her back was to the horses. I watched as Ransom walked up silently behind her and just as he was within reach he snorted loudly. The cat went straight up in the air and hit the ground running. Ransom just turned around and went back to his hay, but I think I could have heard a chuckle if I listened closely enough.

One morning when I went out to feed, Rannie came in from the pasture, and as he neared I smelled the unmistakable odor of skunk. Ransom reeked of the nasty odor, especially his head and face. I believe he probably saw a skunk in the pasture and thought he would startle the skunk as he did the barn cat. He didn't realize skunks have their own way of retaliating for such antics. This horse sense of humor helped Mike and me both as we went about the stresses of life.

At some point, Ransom developed Potomac Horse Fever (PHF), a deadly disease. Ransom's symptoms came on overnight. I called my vet and learned we needed to get antibiotics into Rannie and very quickly, as time was of the essence.

I picked up the antibiotics, syringe, and needles needed to inject the drug, which had the consistency of thick molasses. Mike and I pumped 40cc of this thickness into Ransom's hip daily for five full days. The medicine was so thick, and I had never seen such a huge needle. But Mike and I knew what we had to do to save our boy, and we did it. To say this was a struggle doesn't begin to describe it, but thankfully it worked.

Ransom stabilized, and he actually forgave us for causing him such pain, though it was a while before he let us walk around behind him. The fever that came with PHF caused laminitis in his front hooves, so Mike and I continued to care for him until he slowly came around. Now he has only occasional mild tenderness.

As the years have gone by, Ransom continues to be our very good horse. He gently takes treats from the hands of our grandchildren. He stands so still while we settle the youngest of them on his broad back. He is our sweet boy, our "Handsome Ransom," and will be loved and cared for to his last day.

# Own a Horse? Maybe

## Marian Rizzo

What is it about little girls and horses? Like a lot of kids, when I was a child, I drew pictures of horses. I pretended I owned one. I rode an imaginary steed around our backyard. And when Christmas rolled around one year, I told my parents I wanted a pony. Then I waited with childlike anticipation for the day to arrive.

Early Christmas morning, I burst from my bed and bounded down the stairs in my pajamas. I hurried into the kitchen and peered out the window at our backyard. Snow covered the ground. Icicles hung from our willow tree. But there was no pony.

I was devastated.

We lived in a residential community. We could own a dog or a cat, but no livestock. Yet, to a ten-year-old girl, such a rule didn't make sense. We had a large fenced yard. I figured we could take care of *one* pony.

Disappointed, I continued to hold on to my dream to own a horse someday. Once, when my family went to a fair, I spotted a

Shetland pony standing alone inside a fenced area. No grass grew there. The ground was covered with sand. The pony turned moist brown eyes at me. I figured he was hungry, so I plucked a few blades of grass and shoved them through an opening in the wire fence. He gobbled them up. I plucked a few more. He ate them too.

Then, I stuck my fingers through the opening. He drew close and let me stroke his neck. His hair felt soft, warm, silky. I talked to him in a gentle voice. He rubbed up against my hand. I could have stayed there all day, except my parents were calling me to follow them.

As I walked away, the pony neighed. Had he called my name? I turned for a last look at him. He stretched his neck in my direction. I blinked back a tear and kept going.

Even at that young age, I had connected with a pony in a way that went way beyond the physical. I didn't own him. I hadn't even ridden him. But in that brief encounter, we had bonded.

While that pony had given me a wonderful sense of awe, other horses left me totally baffled.

Like Jake.

It was years later, and I was a teenager. A group of my friends invited me on my first trail ride. By the time we got to the ride center, I was nearly jumping out of my skin with excitement. At last, I was going to ride a horse.

I was matched with Jake, a chestnut quarter horse with a black mane and tail. Most of my friends had ridden before and had no trouble mounting their animals. I needed a boost to get into the saddle. Our guide instructed us on proper rein control. I put a death grip on the horn and merely used the reins as a decoration.

I had heard that horses have a sixth sense about people. They immediately know who's the boss. This time, it wasn't me. Jake took charge the moment I slid my foot in the stirrup. He set off on the trail as if an invisible goad had poked his rump.

During the ride, I found out Jake was antisocial. When another horse came up beside us, Jake's ears went back, and he gave him a good kick with his back hoof. Then he did a little dance that, from where I sat, felt more like bucking. After that, whenever Jake's ears went back, I held on for dear life.

A while later, Jake spotted a cluster of trees. He headed right for them, scooted under the leafy canopy, and tried to use the low-hanging branches to brush me off. I leaned so far back my head rested on his rump.

But I stayed on. My heart pounding, I emerged from under the tree, gripping the horn with one hand and pulling leaves and twigs out of my hair with the other. My friends simply shook their heads and rode away, laughing.

As we continued on the trail with the others, Jake appeared to have settled down. I told everybody to keep their horses away from us. As long as we had the trail to ourselves, Jake behaved. I was beginning to relax when, for no reason, Jake decided it was time to go back to the barn.

He took off like a bolt of lightning. All I could do was hang on, bounce in the saddle, and pray that I wouldn't fall off. I think my backside was sore for a week after.

Surprisingly, that incident didn't dampen my love of horses. Nor did it change my mind about owning one someday. After I married, we settled on a three-acre plot in the country. It looked like my longtime dream to own a horse might come true. But first, I needed to learn everything I could about taking care of one of those big animals.

I decided to volunteer at a local boarding facility. The owner welcomed the extra help. And it was free. Two teenage girls were in charge of the stables. They taught me how much and when to feed the horses. They showed me how to cross-tie a horse and properly groom him. And, they taught me how to muck stalls. From that day on, mucking was my main job.

At the time, four horses occupied the stalls. Two of them—Prince and Barney—were brown with a black mane. They looked exactly alike, except Barney had a white star on his forehead. There were other differences that should have mattered to me. Prince was gentle. Barney was a feisty nipper. Prince was easy to control. Barney had been known to bolt and run off. Many a time, the owner of the farm had to jump in his pickup truck and chase after him.

After a couple of weeks, the two stable girls rarely showed up anymore. Why should they? I was doing their chores.

One day, after I finished the dirty work, I decided to take Prince out of his stall for a little grooming. I cross-tied him in the center of the barn and began to brush his coat. Something didn't seem right. I took a closer look and noticed the white star in the middle of his forehead. I had grabbed Barney by mistake!

With a lump in my throat and my body rigid with anxiety, I slowly but firmly led Barney back to his stall, the whole while murmuring words of comfort in his ear. For some reason, he didn't try to get away. I was amazed. I had controlled a horse. I had shown him who was boss.

Or could it be that a merciful God had looked down from heaven and had seen that I needed help?

Whatever the case, I came away from that experience convinced that I was too skittish and inexperienced to be a good horse owner.

Time passed quickly. My interest turned to raising a family. Soon, I had a daughter who also loved horses. When Joanna was ten years old, I sent her to a horse camp during her summer break from school. She earned several trophies in various categories.

When Joanna's birthday rolled around, we decided to surprise her with a horse of her own. Silky was a Welsh pony/Morgan mix—if you can imagine such a combination. He looked like Black Beauty, except he had a big neck.

While my daughter trotted Silky around the paddock, I leaned against the rail fence and smiled with satisfaction. I finally had a horse, but it really wasn't mine. It was Joanna's. I merely watched from afar and enjoyed the ride vicariously.

Silky was fast. He could take turns like a trained barrel horse. Sometimes, Joanna would take him out of the paddock to adjoining acreage where our neighbor grazed his Arabian horses. From our back porch I had a good view of those gorgeous animals kicking up their heels and frolicking together.

But one day, I would see another side of horses that isn't obvious on the surface. It has nothing to do with speed or stamina or even how pretty they are. It has to do with what's inside.

I saw it the day my ten-year-old granddaughter met Marshmallow, a seventeen-year-old Welsh-Arabian mare, one of the stable buddies at a therapeutic riding facility.

Because of her extreme shyness, Zelda had been having trouble relating to people. Joanna and I prayed that God would show us a way we could help my granddaughter overcome her social anxiety.

Then Joanna remembered the wonderful experiences she'd had at horse camp. Because Zelda also loved horses, we signed her up for equine assisted therapy. The same way I had bonded with the Shetland pony years ago, Zelda immediately connected with Marshmallow.

As time passed, we could see that Zelda's relationship with Marshmallow was helping to bring her out of her shell. Because she had to use verbal commands, Zelda learned to speak loud enough for the horse to hear and obey. Within a few months, my granddaughter blossomed from a shy, noncommunicative child into a confident person. She began to acknowledge her instructors and even repeated their commands. She made the honor roll in school. And she began to open up to people outside of her immediate family.

At the end of the season, the clients performed in a show for family and friends. I was consumed with a grandmother's pride as Zelda guided Marshmallow around the arena, got her up to a gentle trot, and then slowed her down so she could move a ring from one pole to another. Zelda looked like she'd been born in the saddle.

Was I jealous? Maybe a little. Such programs weren't around when I was a child. But I couldn't have enjoyed the show more if I'd been riding the horse myself.

I thank God for answering our prayers and for helping us find a positive outlet for Zelda. Because of that experience, it occurred to me that God didn't create horses merely as a means of transportation. Nor did he create them just for show. I believe when God came up with a design for those magnificent animals, he instilled in them a connection to humans that goes beyond the surface. Zelda has it with Marshmallow. I briefly had it with the Shetland pony. Maybe I even connected with Jake on some level. And possibly with Barney.

Though I never fulfilled my dream to own a horse, I learned over the years that some people are meant to be horse owners. Some are meant to be riders. And some of us are meant to simply admire them from afar.

# The Old Cowboy and a Horse Called Magic

## Tim Fall

Dad grew up in central Washington cattle country. His parents managed a dairy, which meant that even during the Depression there was always food on the table. In his teens Dad worked for a family friend on their cattle ranch riding herd, roping and branding, calving in the spring. A working cowboy and a rodeo cowboy, he and Buff, the rancher, entered competitions as team ropers, heading and heeling.

Dad once said he'd walk a half mile to saddle up a horse in order to ride out and open a gate only a quarter of a mile away. Horses and cattle were his life. Riding and ranching were a good future for someone back in the 1930s. There may not have been much money in it, but the pay was steady and the food was good.

It wasn't all horses and cattle, though. Dad and his older brother could sing and play guitar, which meant they were in demand for singing the cowboy songs that brought people in to the honky-tonk bars on Saturday night. They might have been only high school kids, but they could make some extra cash this way. And then Pearl Harbor got bombed.

Dad turned eighteen less than a week after the attack on Oahu. Dad's high school principal said he had enough units to graduate early, and after getting that paperwork finished, Dad's next stop was the recruiting office. If it weren't for World War II taking him from the cattle country of central Washington to the US airfields of central China, he might have stayed a cowboy. But instead of herding cattle he learned to keep aircraft flying and then made a career of it in Northern California at San Francisco Airport.

Dad's old now. At ninety-four, he stands shorter than the 5′3″ he once boasted as his tallest height. He was living on his own until a couple years ago when he fell in his kitchen and took a bad blow to the head. After an emergency neurosurgery that went into the early morning hours, there was a lengthy period in a rehab hospital. Then he moved to an assisted living apartment near my wife and me.

Dad's health is once again good for a man his age. But he's finding it hard to remember things, especially recent events. He still loves horses, though, and when he found out the local university has an equestrian center, he told me he wanted to visit. Every time we'd get together for coffee or errands, he'd bring it up. I'd been there when they had an open house a few years earlier, so I told him I'd call and ask about taking a tour.

I checked online and found the equestrian center's Facebook page. There was a contact person listed, and I sent a message asking about visitors. She responded almost immediately and encouraged me to bring Dad out. All we needed to do was check in at the office, and they'd get one of the student staff to take us around.

When I told Dad about the trip, he was pleased. He doesn't show as much excitement about things as he used to, and maybe that's a matter of how his brain has been working. But he was clearly looking forward to the trip. We chose a day when the forecast was for sunshine and gentle temperatures.

I picked Dad up and drove onto campus, past the dormitories and football stadium, past the medical school and veterinary hospital, and onto a gravel and dirt road that wound around a bit. We finally pulled into the lane stretching between a couple of fenced pastures and up to the barn housing the tack rooms, some horse stalls, and a small office.

One of the students pulled up on a quad with a pair of hay bales on the back. She stopped next to a shed, unloaded the hay, then walked back toward us.

"Can I help you?"

"We were hoping to look around," I said. "I was told someone might be able to help us out."

Kate, a graduating senior, took us through the barn and by the covered arena, describing the different activities. There was a dressage ring, a green pasture with low fences for hunters and jumpers, a farrier's shed. Only students are permitted to board horses there. No faculty or public horse owners are allowed in an effort to keep costs affordable for the students bringing their horses from home.

The last stop was to see Kate's horse, Magic. He's old, like my dad. And tall, unlike my dad. Dad asked Kate if he could go in the stall.

"Sure. He's very gentle."

Dad stepped in. The top of his head came well below Magic's shoulder. Dad spoke softly to him and reached his hand up to stroke Magic's neck. Magic lowered his head, nuzzled Dad for a moment, then tucked his nose right into Dad's shoulder and left it there.

Magic stood like that for about five minutes, almost cuddling into Dad as Dad stroked his neck and continued to murmur soft words to him. Eventually Dad dropped his hand and stepped out of the stall. "He's a good old horse."

We said thank-you to Kate, who looked pleased to have been able to share her Magic with Dad, and then drove away, back down the lane, onto the gravel road, past the medical school and football stadium, and back into town.

This time the memory stayed with Dad, the day an old cowboy and an old horse shared a moment together.

# Riding Royalty

## *Delores Topliff*

Because Dad was a railroad locomotive engineer, our family could get low-cost rail passes to travel throughout the United States. The summer I turned twelve, Mom decided that she, my little sister, and I should ride what people called an iron horse from Washington State to the upper Midwest to visit relatives on Dad's side of the family. We hadn't met them, but Dad's parents stayed in touch.

For me, the best stop was a large dairy farm near La Crosse, Wisconsin, where Grandpa's sister and her husband lived. I'd never met Great-Aunt Viola, but she and Uncle Art raised nine healthy children on that farm. Their son Wendell was a year older than I and took me to tour the whole farm. I loved the horses most.

Horses of all shapes and sizes belonged to family members, except for Queenie. She was large, white, swaybacked, and the oldest horse so was officially "out to pasture." To me she was beautiful.

I'd only been on a horse once before. That ride in fourth grade came close to being the end of my equestrian career. The owner of two genuine Portland Meadows Racetrack horses boarded them in the pasture next to our elementary school, where they grazed on thick green grass beneath apple trees. Watching them every day through school windows, I daydreamed about riding them. I pictured myself crawling through the fence and climbing into apple tree branches to drop onto a horse for an exciting ride.

By spring, I found three girls willing to help me try. So one day after school, two of us climbed into overhanging apple tree branches while two others got behind the horses and chased them our way. It worked. As the unsuspecting horses passed beneath where two of us hid, we dropped onto their backs and held on.

We weren't experienced riders, so we twisted our hands into their manes. Both horses tried to buck us off, but we stayed seated until they reached the end of the field and slowed to turn around. That's when we slipped off to switch roles so the other girls could ride, but it was not to be.

The horses' owner ran out of the house as soon as he saw us, and my friends and I had our ears blistered with swear words we'd never heard before. Amazingly, nothing happened to us, and we heard no more about it. But we girls dissolved our horse-lover club and stayed clear of that pasture.

Here on our relatives' Wisconsin farm, I could ride horseback legally with a saddle and reins. Mmmm. The creaky leather saddle cousin Wendell lifted from the barn's half wall smelled like heaven—almost as good as the perfect horse he led to me.

"This is Queenie," he said. "Her bridle goes on first." He approached the white horse to slip it over her head while she stood patiently. Next, he placed the heavy saddle over her broad, slightly bowed back, and she stood still for that too. Wendell had brought homegrown carrots from their big garden so I could become Queenie's new best friend. She chomped and nibbled while I stroked her head, and Wendell got his horse ready.

Our first ride was heaven, slow and easy around the farm's rolling landscape with Wendell at my side on his more energetic mare. I gave Queenie rest periods by the stream or pond, and we didn't gallop fast or far enough for her to get worn out. I was sure she loved our time together as much as I did. By the end of that first day, my sitter was sore from being in the saddle so long, and I started walking with a limp. But I didn't care, so that didn't stop me. I continued riding, and after the second day, Wendell left me on my own while he did farm work.

From sunrise to sunset, I stayed in the saddle. Seeing the world from Queenie's broad back, I was royalty that she carried forth. I was a female warrior and she my powerful charger. I was an explorer and she helped me conquer distant realms. I didn't complain when the skin on the inside of my legs wore away from constant rubbing against the saddle. I had regrown new skin from various scrapes plenty of times and would again. I had few days to enjoy Queenie so I made the most of them. Great-Aunt Viola joked that maybe they should hand up meals to me, since I wanted to stay in the saddle.

But our vacation would soon end. How could I live without Queenie?

Maybe I wouldn't have to.

Uncle Art said that because I loved Queenie that much, and she had finished her service years on the farm, maybe I could have her. If I could get her home.

"It's a shame you don't live closer," he said. "Your place is about two thousand miles west. If you can find a way to get Queenie there, I'll give her to you."

"Give her to me?"

That Sunday morning, we attended their church. I sat in a class with Wendell and one of his sisters. Looking back, I'm not sure what the lesson was. I wonder if it mentioned the children of Israel walking from Egypt to the Promised Land. Suddenly, I knew how to keep Queenie. I would ride her home!

It would be easy. I was good at using maps. If we rode west, maybe twenty miles a day for one hundred days, we'd arrive. Of course, we'd stop to see interesting sights like the Badlands and Yellowstone National Park and plan good times to stop and graze. After all, that's how our nation's pioneers traveled west. Many of them walked and survived the long journey. It would be easier yet to ride. Our home was near Fort Vancouver at the end of the Oregon Trail, so I could basically follow the route the pioneers did.

"They didn't all survive," Mom said when she heard my plans.

I borrowed our cousins' World Atlas to start charting.

When Mom called Dad and handed me the phone, he said, "You're only twelve—not old enough."

I was crushed.

"Maybe when she's older," Uncle Art said. Aunt Viola was our blood relative, not him. But since he understood my heart so perfectly, he became my favorite relation. He was a good and wise man. Perhaps being the father of nine children gave him the experience and wisdom to know how to encourage children's dreams.

As a successful dairy farmer, Uncle Art owned his own Piper Cub airplane. He was an excellent pilot and president of Wisconsin's Flying Farmers. "Come on," he said when our days were up. "I'll fly you from here to Mankato to catch your train. You have to ride the iron horse home this time. But I have an idea," he added. "Talk to your folks. Maybe if you come back to see us a year from now, or even two or three, you can ride Queenie home then—if she lives that long."

Seriously?

He nodded. His warm smile showed even Mom he meant it.

A year from now? A year with 365 wonderful days? Even if it took that long, all kinds of amazing things could happen in a year. I could earn money, study more pioneer trails, find perfect maps, assemble a survival kit for Queenie and me—enough plans and possibilities to make our journey work.

I would start today. My grown-up behavior all year long would win my parents' approval. I would make them proud they had raised such a daughter. And maybe earn an advanced Girl Scout badge.

We hugged Aunt Viola and their children good-bye and climbed into Uncle Art's pickup to drive to his farm airstrip. The long runway paralleled Queenie's pasture. As he loaded suitcases into his plane, I waved to her until we climbed inside. Then he closed the door.

"I'll taxi slowly," he said, "so you can say more good-byes." Just then, the late summer thunderstorm that had been forecast blew in. I kept waving so Queenie would know how much I loved her and that I would come back for her. But once Uncle Art revved his engine and began to taxi, solid sheets of wind and pounding rain hit so hard, it was all he could do to keep his plane moving forward. That storm knocked us around like a badminton shuttlecock. We concentrated on staying airborne without getting sick, so there wasn't really time to mourn leaving Queenie behind.

Once we were airborne, I couldn't spot the amazing white horse on the nicest dairy farm we'd ever visited. I left with high hopes that I would see her again and manage to bring her west. But that next spring, we got word that Queenie had died peacefully and entered eternal green pastures. All the same, meeting and loving her taught me that God can always show us ways to make life's best dreams come true.

# Babycakes

## Diane K. Weatherwax

After a handful of lessons and a few hours in the saddle, I decided to buy a horse. After all, riding didn't seem to be that difficult. How much more was there to learn?

So as I approached age forty-five, I bought a four-year-old Appaloosa gelding with thirty days of training. His name was Vinnie. He was thin (looking at him from the front he looked like a fish) and scruffy. I was instantly smitten. Vinnie, not so much.

Two months later I moved him to a boarding facility closer to my home. Kris, the barn owner, promptly fattened him up, and that spring he shedded out to be a very handsome boy—chestnut with a white blanket, four white stockings, and a large white blaze between soft, expressive eyes. As our bond grew, he acquired the loving nickname of Babycakes, complete with my rendition of the song with that name. Riding him was pure joy.

That first summer Vinnie was stricken with Potomac Horse Fever and almost died. He spent five days at Michigan State University's Large Animal Clinic, and upon release was weak and sick but alive. The next few weeks were challenging. He had lost well over a hundred pounds, which he could ill afford. So our goal was simple: slow but steady weight gain and conditioning. Our rides were few and far between.

By fall Vinnie had regained his strength, and I began riding regularly again. I was blessed to have seasoned riders at the barn (many of them cherished friends to this day) who took a novice rider and her green horse under their wings, shared their knowledge, and gave their precious time. Two of them were Barb and Pam.

Barb would have been a regular in *Dressage Today*. She had two gorgeous Hanoverians that required a sensitive, skilled rider. Barb was an expert on outerwear and schooled me on the correct lead at the canter. I didn't care; I was just grateful Vinnie cantered at all. But Barb was undeterred by my foolishness and insisted I stop Vinnie and try again until he picked up the correct lead. I can still picture her, slender and fit in her breeches, hands on her hips with a look of total despair saying, "But Diane, you *must* care." I'm sure my attitude and incompetence gave this sweet woman heartburn.

Pam belonged to a regal Morgan gelding named Nicky who was convinced there were horse-eating monsters everywhere. Pam's calm and quiet leadership was just what Nicky required. Pam had many gifts—she was an excellent educator, gourmet cook, and (my personal favorite) a human instant replay. Never did she miss an incident of Vinnie misbehaving, and she would relay the entire episode in fine detail to his quivering owner, explaining what happened and my heroic response. She was lavish with praise—my own personal cheerleader.

But the most patient of all was my sweet boy, Vinnie. He tolerated my clumsiness and forgave my rigid hands, performing well despite his youth, his limited training, and my inexperience.

As fall turned to winter, Vinnie's sweetness turned to teenager rebellion. He knew I was not a confident rider. He had my number and began testing me. Initially I rode through his behavior until one day he took it to a new level and reared. The Hi Ho Silver kind, only I wasn't the Lone Ranger. To avoid cardiac arrest, I got off. Empowered, he reared every single time I got on. And there was no riding him through it. I was too scared.

One night I sat at the kitchen table, defeated. I had waited my whole life to own a horse, and I adored Vinnie. But my trips to the barn were becoming a nightmare. My fear owned me, and Vinnie knew it. I was mulling over my options, none of them particularly appealing.

My teenage son, Mark, came into the kitchen. "What's wrong?" he asked.

I tried to shrug it off, but he was having none of it. When I admitted how scared I was, he sat down across from me.

Mark played hockey, a sport he loved. He'd started late and struggled the first two years. But he persevered. He went to countless hockey camps and practiced, practiced, practiced. And hockey is rough. He'd broken several bones, dislocated his shoulder, and had his bell rung many times. Now, at seventeen, he had become a commanding presence on the ice, a force to be reckoned with.

"Mom," Mark said, "every time I step on the ice, I'm scared. But I love hockey so much I'm not going to let my fear stop me from doing what I love. You love Vinnie and waited a long time for him. Next time you get on, steel yourself. Leave your fear outside the arena and let your heart take over. If it were easy, everyone could do it." Then he hugged me, raided the fridge, and went back to his homework.

*Wow*, I thought. *Out of the mouths of babes.*

So the next day I got back on Vinnie. Like clockwork he reared. But this time I found my heart. As his feet left the ground I leaned forward in the saddle and popped him between the ears. Stunned, he stopped. With my single decisive act, I became Vinnie's leader, and he never reared again.

I lost my beloved Vinnie in October of 2016. My heart was shattered. Two days after his death I was sorting through our things with the intention of giving most of it away, when I momentarily stepped back from my grief. I had waited almost forty-five years for him. A lifetime. We had twenty years of beautiful memories—some of my happiest moments were with that amazing creature. The young, the old, and the disabled all had a turn riding Vinnie. His photo albums are proof of the many lives he touched—their beaming faces a testament to his sweet, giving nature.

We had had our own private dressage shows, and Vinnie always placed first. His birthday on May 3 was the perfect excuse for a barn party, complete with cupcakes and a large sign on his door proclaiming his greatness. (My personal favorite was "Ask not what Vinnie can do for you, ask what you can do for Vinnie.") He was with me in the best and the worst of times.

The great Winston Churchill once said, "Never give up on something that you can't go a day without thinking about."

No, I decided, I am not going to live the rest of my life without this gift from God we call horses. Forty-five years was plenty long enough.

# One Saturday Morning

## Lonnie Hull DuPont

It was a Saturday morning in January, and I'd just left a doctor appointment a half hour from home. A long bout of bronchitis had taken over my life for several weeks. Even though things had improved physically, I was having trouble feeling it emotionally. Frankly, I was feeling pretty low.

I live in southeastern Michigan, where the sun only shines an average of 111 days per year. Fortunately, this was one of those days—cold and snowy, but sunny. I drove down the interstate toward home flanked by the white brilliance of familiar fields.

Spur of the moment, I decided to exit about twelve miles early. I remembered some friends telling me about a new restaurant on a lake road I never traveled, so I decided to locate it for future use and find my way home from there. I exited, drove to the top of the ramp, and stopped at the stop sign. I saw no traffic in this farming area, which was not unusual—no traffic, except a saddled horse trotting by on the road in front of me. With no rider.

*What?* Where was the rider? The horse was headed north, so I turned my car south to look for a possibly injured human. After a quarter mile of seeing nobody, I realized I'd better deal with the horse on the road with his dangling reins. I quickly U-turned. As I caught up with the horse, I called 911, put my flashers on, and slowed down behind him.

The horse trotted briskly on the correct side of the road, which was good news. When we came to an S curve, however, he strayed to the left. Fortunately, the two pickup trucks that came along saw him in time to avoid him. Then they drove on.

The 911 operator asked me about landmarks, but I had never been on this road before, and I hadn't noted the names of the two side roads I'd passed. "Is the next road Katz Road?" she asked. Yes, there it was, and lo and behold, Mr. Horse made a right turn onto Katz Road. Now it occurred to me that he might be heading to his home. I told the dispatcher that if he stopped, I'd try to get his reins, and I followed the horse down Katz Road.

I grew up with horses, though I'd not dealt with any since I was in high school. I was never much of a horse whisperer. But I knew this guy needed help, and I appeared to be the only help available. He was still moving at a fast trot with dangling reins on Katz Road—a remote road, I was discovering, covered in packed snow over gravel and a little slick. I saw no houses or farms. On either side of the road were woods, some of them down a steep ravine.

The horse began to tire—I'd been following maybe a mile and a half by now, and I could see he was weary. He stopped trotting and walked. Then his feet started to slide a little on the surface. My heart was in my throat until he stopped sliding. The road was narrow with not much for shoulders, and right at the north edge of the road at this spot was a steep ravine. My fear was that he'd stumble or slide into that ravine. But the horse knew he should stop, and there he stood, uneasy, panting, drenched in sweat, facing away from me.

I got out of the car and told the dispatcher, "I'm going to get his reins, but you need to get someone else here, please." I began inching toward the horse and talking quietly. I'd had hip surgery several months ago with some complications, but my adrenaline took away any pain. I kept moving toward the exhausted horse, and he continued to look away from me in the direction of what was most likely home.

Many things scrolled quickly through my mind. I recalled an incident eighteen years ago when I was driving down another country road, and a bareback horse came trotting up the road in the other lane. He had a dangling lead rope. That day, I stopped my car and thought, *I can step out and grab the rope and stop him.* But again, I hadn't been near a horse in decades, and I chickened out as he passed me. Then I saw the owner on a dead run coming up the road. I told him to get in, and we were able to overtake the horse. The owner hopped out of the car, grabbed the lead rope, and did what I'd wanted to do. All was well. But as I drove away, I kicked myself inside. It could have turned out badly, and I should have grabbed that rope. *If that ever happens again,* I said to myself, *I will do what needs to be done.*

Well, here I was.

It took about sixty seconds of sweet talk and slow movement to get within a couple feet of today's horse. Then he turned his head, looked me in the eye, and practically handed me his reins. I took them and began stroking his soaked neck. I reported to the dispatcher, "I have the reins. He really needs to get off this road. You have to send help."

"I have a cruiser on its way," she said.

And so we waited. Who knows where the cruiser was coming from—we were in the middle of nowhere.

I took in my situation. Fifteen minutes ago, I'd been driving home in my ordinary car on an ordinary day through familiar sights and feeling quite blue. Now here I stood on a slick and snowy road

I'd never seen before with no house or human in sight, hanging on to a big strange horse. How did this happen?

I looked my new friend over. He was a trim, handsome bay gelding, English-saddled, and he wore beautifully crafted leather booties over his hooves, something I'd never seen before. Now he started to walk in a tight circle. I remembered one should not relinquish control, so I gave a sharp tug on his reins close to the bridle and firmly said, "Whoa." That worked. For a while. Then we'd do it all over again while I maneuvered not to get stepped on. Clearly he wanted to go home.

It was so quiet on this road surrounded by woods. When was the last time I had been so quiet?

Finally a cruiser showed up. The sheriff, a friendly young woman, got out of the car. She asked how I was doing, then right away told me she knew nothing about horses. Great. "I do know this horse was involved in a hunt today," she said. "They've put the word out for locals to come help."

"Tell me that's going to be soon."

It was not. The sheriff and I chatted while every couple of minutes the horse tried the circling thing. He was getting his groove back. My fear was that he'd decide he was done waiting and start walking me briskly toward his home. I might not be able to stay on my feet on this slick surface. That would not be good. My doctor had told me the first rule of hip surgery recovery is "Don't fall." The second rule is "Obey the first rule."

Then the most beautiful sight appeared—down the road cresting a hill I saw another horse and its female rider. They moved toward us quickly, gracefully, like a vision. My horse turned his head toward the newcomers and seemed cognizant that rescue was in sight. He looked relieved. So relieved that his tail promptly went up and he dropped a significant and sustained pile of manure on the snowy road. The sheriff and I got out of the way and laughed together.

The horsewoman reached us, all smiles. "Thanks so much for this," she said. "His rider is fine. If you hand me the reins, I'll take him—his home is right up the road."

I briefly told the two women about my vow that previous time I'd encountered a horse in the road, that the next time I'd do something.

"You redeemed yourself today, ma'am," said the smiling horsewoman. As she and her mount started up the road, my gelding followed calmly behind, his anxiety clearly quelled. The sheriff and I said our good-byes and got in our vehicles. I watched horse and entourage continue up the road, over a hill, and away.

I realized I was smiling. I had stumbled upon a temporary reprieve from the blues. Sunshine, fresh air, a beautiful horse, a sense of purpose, then victory. All before lunch.

I never got the horse's name. But I am grateful to have met him.

# Coming Back to Myself

## Nicole M. Miller

I t had been one of those weeks—the perfect storm.

Jet lag from ten days in Singapore, one toddler with a cold, an infant with an ear infection, one chicken deceased of unknown causes, and goodness, even the dog had an ear infection.

And then I got a text message—my horse, boarded at a stable thirty minutes away—had a swollen eye.

Well. At least every species in our family was covered, right? (We don't have any cats . . . or goats . . .)

I wasn't sure I could handle one more thing. We'd been in survival mode for the past year since my second child was born, only eighteen months after our firstborn. Between the full-time job, animals, and our infant refusing to sleep through the night, I'd rarely seen my horses at the barn. It seemed impossible to steal the few hours it required.

So after the chaos of bath time, some sort of dinner (the toddler would only drink milk + powdered breakfast mix at this time), and putting both babies to bed, I unburied my cowboy boots from the depths of the closet and left my husband in charge of the baby monitor.

Instantly, the drive—with the car seats in the back empty for a change—was a balm to my weary soul. It dawned on me slowly that I was so relieved for this escape, no matter the reason. Driving through winding roads, listening to music without a toddler screaming, "Mom, Mom, Mom, Mom, Mom!" the entire time, I decided this was worth not getting laundry done.

And then that first step out into the atmosphere rich with the smell of hay, dust, cedar shavings, and warm horses drifted over me. The wind brushed the trees, and horses nickered from their paddocks.

My horse's swollen eye was a concern, yes, but it was a second thought in that moment to the freedom and clarity that the environment brought to me. Life slowed as I moved down the aisle toward my horse's stall. I didn't even attempt to squelch the smile. I recognized this woman. I remembered her. I so rarely got to come back to her.

Here, I moved with confidence. A lifetime spent around horses had emboldened me with that confidence, versus the uncertainty of the wilderness of toddlerhood. Here moments expanded and contracted as I went through the motions, soaked in the smells, reveled in the grit of dirt on my hands.

I relived the years of showing in 4-H when I used the old soft-bristled brush that has lasted me more than a decade. I recalled the glitz and glam and hair spray of two years spent as a rodeo queen when I saw my Miss Teen Rodeo Washington embellished breast collar hanging off my saddle.

I tended to my horse's eye. There was nothing alarming causing the swelling, but I'd need to check on it the next day to ensure it wasn't getting worse.

The next day. A promise of one more day with a "reason" to come. Something to cut through the fog of survival mode and to demand breaking free.

I hurried back as the evening grew later, and though there wasn't time for a ride this time . . . I held out hope.

And that next day came, along with a bit longer of a window for my escape. I saddled up my husband's horse and took to the outdoor arena as the sun dipped into the tree line. I couldn't recall how long it had been since I'd ridden (and ridden without the kids there, demanding so much focus and attention, waiting for their turns).

It happened to be Mother's Day. This first ride in who knows how long.

That ever-present parent guilt raged inside of me. What does it mean that I want to be riding more than anything on the holiday solely dedicated to me as a mother?

Horses have always been my escape—from the figurines as a young girl to my first horse at age twelve to the tales I read and write that all extoll the virtue and beauty of these creatures. And yet they are so much more than an escape.

They keep me grounded. Keep me humble. I am confident in my interactions, yes, but still always ready for the unknown. I've fallen enough to know the role that falling plays in the pursuit of any love, any passion.

And yet, I realize now how I forget that as I'm mired in the day-to-day, that my busy, hectic, beautiful, messy life as a mom of two little boys under the age of three is hard, uncomfortable, and frustrating at times—and yet so was my life with horses. But I'm much further into my horse parenting than I am into human parenting.

It is endurance. It is gratitude.

It is knowing who you are and what the horse needs you to be: consistent and compassionate.

It is a culmination of all my childhood dreams at the same time: seeing my children astride my horses or riding with my husband is more than my heart can even bear sometimes.

I've wondered time and time again if it makes any sense to have two horses while in this unpredictable, turbulent time of raising young kids. I'm not sure—financially it makes little sense, especially given how little time we're able to allot them.

But it is moments like these—where being around or astride my horse centers me, challenges me. These horses are messengers and speak to me in a way I've learned to speak after only so long of listening. If we needed to sell these horses tomorrow, I would not lament this as time lost but rather simply these rare and deep moments where I rediscovered the girl I was and the woman I hope to be.

I realized there was no shame in wanting to spend my Mother's Day with the animals who formed me into the mother I am.

Until the next time, my steadfast companions.

# A Real Enough Horse

## Karen Foster

"Can I have a horse?" I begged my daddy. I was eleven years old and in love with the idea of owning a horse.

My family lived in Tucson, Arizona, at the time. Surrounded by mountains and a pastel desert filled with cacti and rolling tumbleweeds, our town was a popular film location for Western movies. Each February, we'd celebrate "La Fiesta de los Vaqueros" (Celebration of the Cowboys), which included the largest outdoor midwinter rodeo in the nation. How could I not love horses? They were a definitive part of the landscape. And I wanted one desperately.

However, living in the "Wild West" in the late 1960s didn't convince my dad that his only daughter needed a horse. Just as the cowgirl in me wasn't deterred by the fact that our family lived in military housing on the Air Force base.

"Why can't I have a horse?" I asked.

"I can buy you a horse," Daddy said. "What I can't afford is the horse's food, boarding, and a veterinarian if he gets ill. I'd also have to drive you to the stables so you could ride him. Then we'd have to sell the horse when we moved."

Okay, so maybe I hadn't thought it through. I went outside to play with my tetherball and came up with plan B.

I read books like *National Velvet* and *Black Beauty*. I studied *Horse Lover's Magazine* in case my dream ever came true. I pretended my bike was a pinto like the horse that Little Joe rode in the television show *Bonanza*. I'd race my imaginary horse around our cul-de-sac with a twig for my riding stick and my head floating in the clouds.

But my greatest joy was collecting miniature horse models. Some of them were expensive and intricately sculptured to resemble their real-life breed such as a palomino. Other horses in my herd were the size of my palm. They came with my younger brother's frontier set. Regardless of their size or value, I named each horse and positioned them on my metal bookcase when I wasn't playing with them. They watched me while I did my homework. Guarded me when I slept.

Their presence comforted me in between friends.

As a military brat, I never settled in one place for long. Our family moved multiple times as I was growing up. Even in Tucson, we'd rented a home for two years before we moved into military housing on base. It was a short distance, but it meant enrolling in a different school. Being the new kid in the neighborhood. And making friends—again.

Not a problem, if you're an extrovert. I recall my mom telling me that kids might interpret my shyness for being stuck-up. I needed to act friendly. Sidle up to a new face instead of waiting for someone to approach me. However, I found it easier to stick my nose in a book and read about someone else's life than navigate new friendships.

The base library became my second home. I could live vicariously through a fictional character like Velvet, who disguised herself as a boy so she could compete in a horse race. I'd embedded myself in stories about famous horses like Bucephalus. When Alexander the Great was a boy, he tamed Bucephalus, and the two of them went together on every fighting campaign. I wept when I read Bucephalus died in battle. And I envied the close-knit bond between the two of them. The friends I made were temporary fixtures because most of them were military brats too. One of us would eventually move away.

I'd read that horses are not loners by nature. They like to have another horse around for companionship. Thoroughbred horses in particular rely on companion ponies for friendship and support. If something happens to the racehorse on the track, the companion pony, which the thoroughbred respects and trusts, inches in and offers reassurance while the horse is in a vulnerable state. If a thoroughbred runs off the course, the companion pony is the one who bounds after him.

Perhaps deep down, I wanted a horse so I could have a loyal companion. Someone I could trust and rely on no matter what. A companion to reassure me when I felt vulnerable. Or maybe I just loved horses like many girls that age. Horses were a combination of beauty, gentility, and power. I only know my horse phase carried me through those insecure adolescent years.

When I entered high school, my passion for horses waned. Baby-sitting, boy fever, and listening to Simon and Garfunkel records took their place. I wrapped my horse models in tissue paper and stored them in a cardboard box that stayed in my closet, next to the white Hullabaloo boots I'd outgrown.

Each time our family moved, the box went with us. However, my horses stayed in their cramped quarters. They never saw the light of day. After college, I got married and brought my precious cargo with me. Almost forty years passed before I opened that musty box. As I carefully unwrapped each horse, my heart skipped. Memories engulfed me. I lovingly ran my fingers over the horses' sculpted muscles. Stroked their smooth backs. I even remembered some of their names.

"Hello, Bucephalus. You've aged well," I told him. "You're still just as handsome."

Those horses had been my companions when I was a youth, but what purpose did they serve now? I needed to downsize. I told myself to find them a new home. Perhaps a little girl would play with them instead of laying them to rest. But the thought of giving away my horses felt akin to losing part of my childhood. What else did I have to show for those adolescent years? The Hullabaloo boots and most of my LP records were gone.

Sentimental tears watered my eyes. I couldn't let go. Not yet. I left my horse models out for a week so I could admire them. Then I wrapped them up like fragile Christmas ornaments and placed them back in the box along with my horse-scented memories.

One of those tucked-away memories is of an eleven-year-old girl clinging to the mane of a horse as they galloped along a white beach, kicking up sand and a frothy surf. Who cares if it was only a young girl's imagination. That horse felt real enough to make her smile. It still does.

# Notes

1. William Shakespeare, *Henry V*, Act 3, scene 7.
2. "Top 10 Smartest Animals," HowStuffWorks.com, https://animals.howstuff works.com/animal-facts/10-smartest-animals.htm.
3. "How to Ride Side Saddle Like a Victorian Lady," https://www.youtube .com/watch?v=RV_oYU5f-8o; Penny Skinner, "The History of the Side Saddle," *Owlcation*, https://owlcation.com/humanities/The-Side-Saddle.
4. https://en.wikipedia.org/wiki/Cincinnati_(horse).
5. www.historynet.com/robert-e-lees-horse-traveller.htm.

# About the Contributors

**Tamera Alexander** (www.TameraAlexander.com) is a *USA Today* bestselling author and one of today's most popular writers of inspirational historical romance. She lives in Nashville, Tennessee, with her husband, not far from the Southern mansions that serve as the backdrop for many of her critically acclaimed novels, including the Belle Meade Plantation series, which features a hero, a heroine—and a horse—in each book. For the past thirty years, every thoroughbred that's raced in the Kentucky Derby traces its lineage back to Belle Meade, but without one man, Robert "Uncle Bob" Green, Belle Meade would not have been the nation's premiere stud farm in the nineteenth century. Uncle Bob was an African American slave, a real-life horse whisperer, and is now a beloved character in each of Tamera's Belle Meade Plantation novels.

**Sarah Barnum** is a freelance editor with a passion for writing and riding. After a career managing a therapeutic riding program for children with special needs, she started TrailBlaze Writing & Editing (www.trail-blazes.com). Sarah enjoys ranch life in Northern

California with her graphic designer husband and her Appaloosa horse, Ransom.

**Cynthia Beach** is an English professor and writer. Her articles and contributions appear in newspapers, literary journals, and books like *Hope in the Mourning Bible* and *The Horse of My Heart*. She cofounded the two-day Breathe Christian Writers Conference and is marketing her novel, *The Seduction of Pastor Goodman*. Her writing how-to, *Creative Juices: A Splash of Story Craft, Process & Creative Soul Care*, is available at cynthiabeach.com.

**Lisa Begin-Kruysman** writes about all things canine from her waterfront studio at the New Jersey Coast. Although she's inspired by the beauty and grace of equines, she's always been a bit intimidated by their stature and power, unlike her late sister, Manette, aka "The Young Horse Whisperer." In honor of her sister's life and love of horses, the author was inspired to share this sweet family memory of a time spent with a special animal. To learn more about her work, please visit www.lisabegin-kruysmanauthor.com.

**Catherine Ulrich Brakefield** says, "My readers inspire my writing." She is the author of five faith-based historical romances: *Wilted Dandelions* and the four-book Destiny series, *Swept into Destiny*, *Destiny's Whirlwind*, *Destiny of Heart*, and *Waltz with Destiny*. She's written two pictorial history books and numerous short stories. See www.CatherineUlrichBrakefield.com for more information.

**Sandy Cathcart** is an artist, writer, and photographer who loves her Creator and all things wild. She lives in the highlands of Oregon with her husband the Cat Man and is the creator of "Capturing Story," an online writing adventure for people who want to leave their stories for generations to come. She is the author of several books, including *Songs in the Night* and *Creator: The Heart of a*

*Lion.* (sandycathcart.com; www.capturingstory.com; sandycath cart(@gmail.com)

**Lonnie Hull DuPont** is an award-winning poet, editor, and author of several nonfiction books. Her poetry can be read in dozens of periodicals and literary journals, and her work has been nominated for a Pushcart Prize. Her nonfiction is frequently about animals, and her most recent book is a memoir of sorts, *Kit Kat & Lucy: The Country Cats Who Changed a City Girl's World*. She lives in southern Michigan.

**Loretta Eidson** writes romantic suspense. She won first place in romantic suspense in the Foundations Awards at the 2018 Blue Ridge Mountain Christian Conference, was a finalist in ACFW's 2018 Genesis Awards, and was a double finalist in the 2017 Daphne du Maurier Award for Excellence. Loretta lives in North Mississippi with her husband, Kenneth, a retired Memphis police captain. She loves salted caramel lava cake, dark chocolate, and caramel frappaccinos.

**Tim Fall** is a California native who changed his major three times, switched colleges four times, and took six years to get a bachelor's degree in a subject he's never been called on to use professionally. He's been married for over thirty years and has an adult son and daughter; his family is constant evidence of God's abundant blessings in his life. He and his wife live in Northern California.

**Susy Flory** (www.susyflory.com) is a *New York Times* bestselling writer. She directs the West Coast Christian Writers Conference near San Francisco and recently started a master's degree at Northern Seminary. Susy loves to help her daughter, Teddy, a wildlife rehabilitator, with an official squirrel nursery currently situated in the laundry room. Their retired thoroughbred racehorse, Stetson, lives nearby.

**Karen Foster** writes true first-person stories about her life, as well as providing a voice on paper for the heroic people she meets. Her story "Tender Mercies" appeared in *Chicken Soup for the Soul: Military Families* (May 2017). Karen also speaks at women's church events and MOPS (Mothers of Preschoolers) about nurturing one's faith and female friendships. You can read her blog or contact her via KarenFosterMinistry.com.

**Susan Friedland-Smith,** author of *Horses Adored and Men Endured* and equestrian blogger at Saddle Seeks Horse, is a middle school history teacher by day and horse girl 24/7. The displaced midwesterner who resides in California writes about real horse life featuring alfalfa scraps in her handbag, always dusty riding boots, and product reviews for horse and rider. Trot along with Susan and her handsome thoroughbred Knight at saddleseekshorse.com and @SaddleSeeksHorse on Facebook and Instagram.

**Yvonne Haislip** lives on forty-four acres in rural Michigan where she tends her gardens and enjoys her animals—chickens, two horses, three dogs (a Great Dane, a mastiff, and a Yorkie), and the wildlife living around her (including an occasional visiting raccoon named Jasper). Yvonne and her husband of many years have five children and one grandchild.

Out of the abundance of her heart, **Tracy Joy Jones** writes, speaks, blogs, and takes her readers on adventures in love and laughter. Tracy and her husband own Jones House Creative, a graphic design firm, where she has the joy of helping other authors tell their stories. In her free time, she reads voraciously, gardens, laughs at every opportunity, and travels as often as she can, while raising her three kids in Jenks, Oklahoma. She'd love to connect with you through her website, www.tracyjoyjones.com, or on her author page on Facebook, https://www.facebook.com/TracyJoyJones Author/. Happy riding!

**Jenny Lynn Keller** is an award-winning author who especially loves transforming her appreciation for the people and places of southern Appalachia into inspirational stories about love, faith, and forgiveness. Her personal story is highlighted at https://www.jennylynnkeller.com/ and her weekly inspirational posts appear at https://www.facebook.com/jennylynnkeller/ and https://www.jennylynnkeller.com/blog.

After retiring from a career in marketing and public relations, **Chris Kent** (bruleridge@gmail.com) and her husband moved to a remote area of the Upper Peninsula of Michigan, where they live with their two quarter horses and a German shorthair. Chris belongs to a group of North Woods writers and has been published in *Equus* magazine. She enjoys gardening, making maple syrup, raising bees, traveling, horseback riding, and volunteering in the community. Sharing a love of nature and animals is a highlight when children and grandchildren visit the Kents' north country retreat.

**Tisha Martin** is an editor by day and a writer by night. Sadly, she no longer owns horses, but they do appear in her historical fiction set on the American home front. Join in the journey: www.tishamartin.com.

**Nicole M. Miller** is the team engagement manager at Buffer, a writer, and an urban homesteader. She lives with her husband, two sons, and an assortment of dogs, horses, and chickens in southwest Washington. Connect with her on Twitter at @nmillerbooks or Instagram at @nicolemillerbooks.

**Karen Lynn Nolan** is an award-winning writer of Appalachian fiction, mystery/suspense, and memoir. Her years in the eastern Kentucky mountains instilled a love of storytelling, mystery, humor, stubbornness, and deep faith. She is the author of *Above the Fog*, set in the Kentucky coalfields, and has contributed to several anthologies. You can connect with Karen at karenlynnnolan.com, karenlynnnolan on Instagram, @karenlynnnolan on Twitter, and karenlynnnolan on Pinterest.

**DJ Perry** (www.djperryblog.com) is the CEO of cdiproductions .com, an American motion picture company. Several of his screenplays have been produced into award-winning films, including the Quest Trilogy (*Forty Nights, Chasing the Star, The Christ Slayer*), *Wild Faith,* and *Man's Best Friend* just to name a few. Additionally, several of his screenplays have been novelized into books. *The Horse of My Dreams* contributions represent DJ's initial steps on his path of writing his own books.

**Sarah Parshall Perry** is the coauthor of *When the Fairy Dust Settles: A Mother and Her Daughter Discuss What Really Matters* (Warner Faith), the author of *Sand in My Sandwich (and Other Motherhood Messes I'm Learning to Love)* (Revell), and the author of *Mommy Needs a Raise (Because Quitting's Not an Option)* (Revell). She writes about more serious things at *The Stream,* Christianitytoday.com, *The Federalist, Christian Post,* and CNS News, among others. Sarah has a JD from the University of Virginia School of Law and enjoys an extraordinary, ordinary life in Maryland farm country with one husband, three kids, five animals, and never enough time. Follow her family's adventures at facebook.com/sarahperryauthor or at instagram .com/sarahpperry.

**Shannon Moore Redmon** writes romantic suspense stories to entertain and to share her faith. Her stories dive into the healthcare environment, where Shannon holds over twenty years of experience as a registered medical sonographer and educator. She is a guest blogger for Jordyn Redwood's *Medical Edge* blog, and her flash fiction stories have been published in *Splickety* magazine. She is a member of the ACFW and Blue Ridge Mountain Writers

Group, and is represented by Tamela Hancock Murray of the Steve Laube Agency. She would love to connect with you at www .shannonredmon.com, Facebook: Shannon Moore Redmon, Twitter: @shannon_redmon, LinkedIn: Shannon Redmon, and Instagram: slmredmon.

**Rachel Anne Ridge** is the author of *Flash: The Homeless Donkey Who Taught Me about Life, Faith, and Second Chances* and *Walking with Henry: Big Lessons from a Little Donkey on Faith, Friendship, and Finding Your Path*. She and her husband live in Texas and are parents of three grown kids and grandparents of five. You can find her online at rachelanneridge.com, and you can keep up with Flash and Henry on Facebook at Facebook.com /flashthedonkey and Instagram at @flashandhenry.

Pulitzer Prize nominee **Marian Rizzo** has won numerous writing awards for her work in journalism and for her novel manuscripts. Her Great Depression era novel, *Angela's Treasures*, was published by WordCrafts Press. To this day, Marian still does not own a horse, but she loves them dearly. Visit Marian at her website, marianscorner.com.

**Lauraine Snelling** is the award-winning author of over seventy novels, including the beloved Red River of the North series. When not writing she can be found paintbrush in hand, creating flowers and landscapes. She and her husband, Wayne, live in the Tehachapi Mountains in California with their basset, Annie, and two Buff Orpington hens, Maud and Mable.

**Claudia Wolfe St. Clair** is an artist, writer, art therapist, and *anam cara* from Toledo, Ohio. A history buff all of her life and a retired reenactor, she now enjoys life in her old family home on Lake Erie. You can read more from her in the Callie Smith Grant collections *Second-Chance Dogs* and *The Horse of My Heart*.

A citizen of both the United States and Canada, **Delores Topliff** loves scenery and landscapes anywhere, plus family, grandchildren, friends, college teaching, mission trips, travel, and her homes in Minnesota and in Mississippi. She enjoys wildlife, gives convincing moose calls, and makes jewelry from just about anything, including porcupine quills. She has four published children's books plus historic novels now offered by the Seymour Literary Agency. Follow her at Delores Topliff on Facebook and delorestopliff.com, or her blog at mbtponderers.blogspot.com.

**Diane K. Weatherwax** is a retired legal secretary who is a member of various animal rights organizations and who has served on her local nonprofit humane society's board of directors. Animals are her passion, and she advocates for them all, wild or domesticated. She was crazy for horses as a kid but never had one until Babycakes, and owning him was a blessing she will never take for granted.

**Connie Webster** has been an animal lover since childhood. She lives in rural Michigan on the same farm where she grew up and raised her children. When she isn't riding trails with her friends or exploring the countryside with her grandkids, she adventures with her husband and tends her bees, horses, dogs, and one elusive cat.

# About the Editor

**Callie Smith Grant** enjoys animals of all kinds. She is the author of many published animal stories, the author of several books for young readers, and the compiler of the anthologies *Second-Chance Dogs*, *The Horse of My Heart*, *The Dog Next Door*, *The Cat in the Window*, *The Dog at My Feet*, and *The Cat in My Lap*.

# Acknowledgments

Many thanks to my brilliant animal-loving editor, Dr. Vicki Crumpton. More thanks to the entire team at Revell, a division of Baker Publishing Group—amazing editors, marketers, designers, warehouse workers, and salespeople. And a very special big thanks to the talented contributors in this book who trust us all with their stories.

# If this hound could like us,
# and trust us, well . . . maybe we could
# trust ourselves.

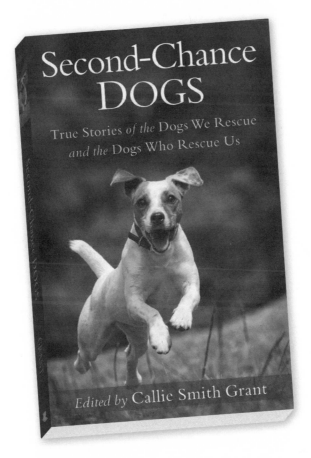

Each of us needs to be rescued from something—and each of us has
the capacity to rescue someone, or something, else. This feel-good
collection of more than thirty contemporary, true stories spotlights
the beauty of being rescued—dogs rescued by people, people rescued
by dogs, and even dogs who rescue other animals.

**Few creatures are as noble and soul-stirring as the horse. They give us a taste of wildness and yet make us feel at home.**

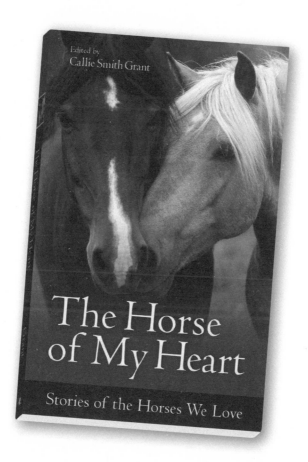

This beautiful collection of stories will inspire and move us in the same way these marvelous beasts capture our hearts and imagination.

# Enjoy These Uplifting Tales of the Cats **We Love**

In this charming collection of true stories, you will find cats of all shapes, sizes, and demeanors. Each of them has played an important part in the lives of their humans. So grab a cup of coffee, find a comfortable chair, curl up with the special cat in your life, and enjoy these uplifting tales.

A PLAYFUL bat of a string. A BORED yawn. A TENDER purr at the touch of your hand.

*The Cat in the Window* is a delightful collection of true stories that celebrate the cats in our lives.

# A WAGGING tail. A GOOFY, floppy-tongued smile. An EXCITED bark when your keys jingle in the door.

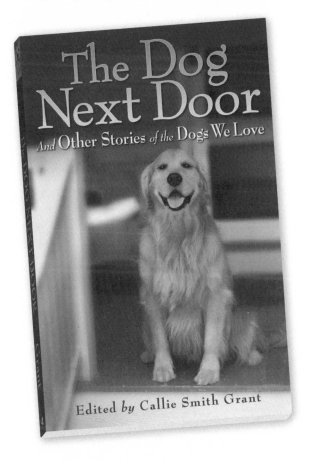

The Dog Next Door is a delightful collection of true stories that celebrate the dogs in our lives.